The
JOYCEAN WAY

A Topographic Guide to
'Dubliners' &
'A Portrait of the Artist as a Young Man'

with maps & photographs

The
JOYCEAN WAY

A Topographic Guide to
'Dubliners' &
'A Portrait of the Artist as a Young Man'

with maps & photographs

BRUCE BIDWELL & LINDA HEFFER

THE JOHNS HOPKINS UNIVERSITY PRESS

BALTIMORE, MARYLAND

First published in the United States of America, 1982,
by The Johns Hopkins University Press, Baltimore, Maryland 21218

ISBN 0-8018-2879-1

LC Number 82-80660

British Library Cataloguing in Publication Data

Bidwell, Bruce
    The Joycean way.
    1. Joyce, James, *1822-1941* —
    Criticism and interpretation
    I. Title   II. Heffer, Linda
    823'. 912   PR6019.09Z/

Printed in the Republic of Ireland
by E. & T. O'Brien Ltd.,
Barrow Street, Dublin.

Acknowledgments:

Quotations where used are from the texts cited in the bibliography, which we gratefully acknowledge. We wish to thank in particular The National Library of Ireland for assistance and permissions with some of the photographs. If we have inadvertantly used other copyright material, we would be grateful if the owners would write to the publisher. We are grateful to Elizabeth Ryan for drawing the maps. The Cover design by Jarlath Hayes. The Joyce cartoon on the cover is copyright Desmond Harmsworth.

CONTENTS

List of Maps and Diagrams

NOTE ON THE MAPS

The maps in this study are based on the Ordnance Survey of contemporary Dublin with the following exceptions and alterations:

(1)   When streets which Joyce mentions in his text have been renamed the present name appears first on the map followed by the turn-of-century name in parentheses: thus, Parnell (Great Britain) Street on Map 4.

(2)   In certain areas of the city and suburbs where reconstruction has obliterated or obscured the arrangement of streets as Joyce knew them, and *where this arrangement is important in visualizing the topography of a given episode*, the maps represent the streets as they existed in Joyce's day. This can be seen in Map 5 of Blackrock (1892), in Map 8 of the Monto District (1895), in Map 13 of Millbourne Lane (1890), and in the representations of Fairview (1900) on Map 14 and of the North Wall Quay and Ringsend (1895) on Maps 21 and 22. In these cases, the maps have been drawn from records available in the Tax Evaluer's Office in Dublin and from information found in *Thom's Dublin Directories* and in the *Ward and Lock Guides* to Ireland.

(3)   Landmarks and buildings to which Joyce refers in his text are shown on the maps as they existed in his day.

(4)   Figure 1, the sketch of Clongowes Wood College, is as it was when Joyce attended the school and is based on information and photographs from *The Clongowes Record: 1814-1932* and on information provided by Roland Burke-Savage, S.J. Figure 2, Belvedere College, is from a photograph in *The Belvederian* (1907). Map 9 represents Cork City as it appeared in the 1890s and is based on information from the *City and County Cork Almanac: 1889-1922*. The sketches are by Linda Heffer.

NOTE ON THE PHOTOGRAPHS

Photographs are by the authors, except where otherwise stated. E.g. 'Lawrence' in the caption indicates the source — The Lawrence Collection (c. 1890-1910) from the National Library of Ireland by kind permission.

Introduction

Part I of *The Joycean Way* deals with *A Portrait of the Artist as a Young Man*; Part II concentrates on *Dubliners*, though the wider reader of James Joyce will recognise features of one or the other of these works which become part of the landscape of Joyce's later fiction, or which are amplified by what is later revealed. Bob Doran's story, for example, only begins on Hardwick Street: the essence of his experience is carried through to *Ulysses*, and as we watch Bloom watch Doran slip into the Empire pub, we are not surprised, knowing Joyce, to look up and find 'Adam's Court' printed above the alley. On the other hand, when Father Flynn's expressed last wish, to visit Irishtown, is unfulfilled, we may learn to our satisfaction in *Ulysses* that it was 'a fine old custom' to route a funeral procession through this district and that, at least, the 'solemn and truculent' corpse was able to go.

We speak here of an actual as well as a creative map, a scheme in which Stephen Dedalus's last meeting with Davin in North Frederick Street on the eve of Stephen's departure takes place within hailing distance of nearly 'everybody': Mrs Mooney in Hardwicke Street, the Sisters in Great Britain Street, Corely and Lenehan passing by on their way to Rutland Square, the Conroys alighting in front of the Gresham Hotel, the mourners following behind Dingham to Glasnevin.

The purpose of this study is to detail as precisely as possible the topography relating to James Joyce's early fictional work. Each section contains large-scale maps showing the placement and movement of all the central characters along with commentary relating the topographical texture to surface theme, and the whole concludes with a complete glossary of the place-names appearing in the two books, indexed for reference to the thirty-eight maps included.

Begun initially as a simple aid to the Dublin tourist in search of Joyceana, our research soon started to suggest that there was a good deal to be said of a critical nature about Joyce's use of the topographical details which surround his characters' movements. Sometimes these details are clearly stated in the stories, and in these cases it is our task to provide gloss and comment for the reader unfamiliar with Dublin and its environs as they existed in 1900. Often, however, Joyce leaves these details unstated (most would be part of the average Dubliner's experience and memory at the time Joyce wrote) though they tend to contribute to the major structural motifs and, in several cases, even seem essential to a full appreciation and understanding of a given episode or story. Time and again, the quality of the characters' movements, the proximity of waterways or waste grounds, the names of streets and shops and pubs, the historical, mythical and biographical associations with place create a texture and environment appropriate to the narrative line. We must conclude that Joyce's surface naturalism in the imaginative use of the real places he knew was of more importance to his particular creative genius than has hitherto been noted. This book, therefore, is a study of Joyce's technique — not his technique of composition, about which much has been written, but rather a source book towards a further examination of the way his imagination functioned as he formed an ordered artistic whole from the chaos of reality.

In completing the research there are many to whom we have become indebted. To begin with, we owe a great deal to Richard Ellmann's *James Joyce* which served as a starting-point and a guide for many of the trails we followed. Without that book always at hand during the early stages, it is safe to say that our task would have been next to impossible.

As we moved towards a reconstruction of the topography of Dublin in 1900, the National Library in Dublin, with its collection of city directories, newspapers and guide-books, became invaluable. The staff there was always friendly and helpful as was the records department of the Tax Evaluer's Office where extremely detailed maps of Joyce's Dublin are housed. The libraries of Trinity College, Dublin, and Cornell University, Ithaca, New York, are also to be thanked for opening their collections to us.

In walking the trail of all of Joyce's characters, we were continually surprised and pleased by the courteous reception the citizens of Dublin accorded to two Americans who imposed on their time with cameras and notebooks: the families now living in residences Joyce left long ago who invited us in for tea and showed us into back rooms and back gardens which would have otherwise been closed to us; those on the streets of Dublin and Bray and Blackrock who would pause to give us directions and advice when we were looking for roads which had been renamed or buildings which no longer existed; Messrs Eamon and Malachy O'Brien who generously showed us materials they had collected; Roland Burke-Savage, S.J., of Clongowes Wood College, who patiently answered all of our inquiries and took the time to show us the College and the grounds; the manager of the seed merchant's office at 15 Usher's Island who allowed us to photograph the setting of 'The Dead', and the guard at the site of the Old National University of Ireland who pointed out the physics theatre and let us walk around the halls and grounds of that building; and especially the bus conductors, shop keepers, bar tenders and friends we made in Donegal, in Ballybofey, in Stranorlar, in Cork, in Galway, in Dun Laoghaire and in Mount Merrion, who were prepared to share their knowledge of Ireland with us and who made the preparation of this book a pleasant experience.

Finally, we would like to thank Seamus Cashman of Wolfhound Press and Maurice Harmon of University College, Dublin, without whose encouragement and advice we would not have begun this project at all.

PART ONE
A PORTRAIT OF THE ARTIST
AS A YOUNG MAN

Preface

'The book's pattern', Joyce told his brother Stanislaus about *A Portrait,* 'is that we are what we were; our maturity is an extension of our childhood. . . .' Because time is condensed and events often transposed, it is unwise to take the novel as scrupulously autobiographical. We are, of course, looking at experience which has been worked through, considered, and reordered to Joyce's own ends. But the artist's highly retentive mind and his sedulous regard for and interest in detail lead us to view Stephen Dedalus's surroundings with as much care as Joyce himself did. His purpose was not only, as Richard Ellmann says, to plunge back into his own past, to justify and to expose it; it was to illuminate a process according to his own aesthetics, to precisely frame and define it, and to make it art.

Joyce said art is 'the human disposition of sensible or intelligible matter for an aesthetic end'. Towards this end he came to rely on actual experience. We watch Stephen in *A Portrait* move from a quest for ideal beauty in a faery world to a quest for beauty arising out of mundane material, which, he decides, gives the artist limitless scope. Despite the emotional chaos of much of his early life, his instincts quite early show the direction he will take. Sitting in the study hall at Clongowes Wood, Stephen looks at the flyleaf of his geography which he had inscribed with 'himself, his name, and where he was'.

Much later he describes to Lynch the three phases of artistic apprehension: wholeness, in which the viewer separates one thing from all other things; harmony, wherein the viewer analyses and feels the rhythm of the thing apprended — sees it 'made of its parts, the result of its parts and their sum'; and radiance, the essence or 'whatness' of the thing, which dawns upon the viewer 'a luminous silent stasis of aesthetic pleasure'. No closer analysis of what makes *A Portrait* work is possible. Stephen and Joyce were interested in creating art, and because life, upon which they draw, is disorderly, it is only through precise definition, analysis and synthesis that they can 'convert the bread of everyday life into something that lives a permanent artistic life of its own'.

The topographical underpinnings of *A Portrait* are drawn from the point of view of the growing Stephen and are subject therefore to the degree of control Stephen has over his surroundings, as well as Joyce's overall artistic control. In Chapter One of the novel Stephen is, by virtue of his age and inexperience, entirely at the mercy of his environment, and, throughout, the preponderant feeling is one of restriction, imposition, the channelling or harnessing of movement. More important than the exact location and direction of events, which plays an important symbolic part in later chapters, is that a great deal of Stephen's activity takes place inside and involves passing from place to place, through corridors or sitting in rooms. The scenes which occur outdoors are also strictly limited, by the parameters of the playing field, by cars or trains, by the strictures of ceremony or the masters' supervision. Joyce takes care to show that these restrictions do not have a salubrious effect on the boy Stephen. The atmosphere at Clongowes is gloomy, ill-lit, dank and cold. The out-of-doors presents dangers within its own limits. Stephen is knocked down and breaks his glasses on the cinder path which leads to his being punished and is pushed into the square ditch which leads to his illness. Such escapes from restriction as are made by Moonan and Tusker and the fellows in the higher line result in some ill-understood transgression and punishment. Stephen's single self-motivated action, going to see the rector about the pandying, brings a sense of pride and achievement, and even as the incident progresses we see a change in the physical surroundings from inauspicious to heroic to congenial (Joyce uses this same technique elsewhere in the novel as well: during the Church Street episode in Chapter Three for example). In Blackrock he is under similar constraints and his activity is largely repetitive: he covers the same route each day with Uncle Charles, runs the same track over and over in the park, follows the same roads on the Sunday walks. Even out of the immediate purvue of his family he plays on the same streets and goes on the same milk run, though, towards the end, a vague disquietude impels him into the evening streets alone.

Nearly all the movement in Chapters Two and Three has a feverish quality which is heightened by the fact that it takes place in the city, amid all the stress and disorder that characterizes this setting. Stephen is free to move as he pleases but he is now driven by confusion or excess of feeling that leaves him at first overwhelmed by his surroundings and later unaware, much of the time, of where he is. When Stephen is composed and sure of himself, Joyce is precise with regard to location. On the evening of the Whitsuntide play, Stephen is relaxed, equanimous, and Joyce depicts the college with thoroughness and precision. After the play when the boy is overcome by his anger and frustration, he sets out down North Great George's Street 'hardly knowing where he was walking'. We don't know where he is until his anger and resentment fall away. Likewise, as Stephen collects his prize money

he maintains his calm and we see exactly where he is, in Foster Place and the Bank of Ireland, and where he is going. After the money and the order which it made possible are gone, Stephen is again beset by isolation and restlessness and his forays into the prostitute quarter are delineated as to mood, but not as to location. The ultimate expression of both temporal and spiritual control results in the bleak and fearful walk towards Church Street. Here again, in his preoccupation with his guilt, Stephen notices only the quality of the air until consciousness of place returns and Joyce places him amidst the squalor of the old streets near the Capuchin Church.

The beginning of Chapter Four is taken up with the fervour of Stephen's religious renewal. Place takes no part in the narrative as Stephen's whole frame of reference is spiritual and his actions other-directed. Once Joyce has him reassert his self, he puts him in closer touch with his surroundings. Both the walk home after the meeting with the director and the walk to the Bull which culminates with his commitment to life and art are relatively specific with regard to place, both because of its important symbolic relevance to the narrative and because Stephen can now interact with his environment, rather than simply react to it.

In Chapter Five we see that Stephen has mastered his environment to the extent that it is subject to his intellection, and certain landmarks appear as direct antecedents to the thoughts and emotions they arouse. Place is now almost entirely concrete and no less a part of Joyce's imaginative repertoire than the numerous biographical sketches, incidents and insights which also find their way into the narrative. Stephen himself is aware of the creative possibilities inherent in his surroundings, and has achieved the control and the distance necessary to make them work.

Chapter One

THE CIRCULAR TRACK

Martello Terrace, Bray (pp. 7-8; 27-39)

From the spring of 1887 through the beginning of 1892, the Joyces lived at Martello Terrace, Bray, in the first of eight arcaded houses which face south towards the massive wrinkled brow of Bray Head. The sea wall is so close to the row of houses that when the wind is fresh, the spray blows into the porch of number one and sea water fills the troughs between the ocean and the strand. During strong easterly gales the Strand Road itself was flooded since, before the creation of the wall and esplanade in the second half of the nineteenth century, it had been merely shingle and dunes, buffeted by waves to the sea's natural extent, the rising ground on the west side of the strand. Behind Martello Terrace a small harbour lay between two piers, one built out from the side of the terrace and one behind, so that it was not uncommon for the Joyce home to be surrounded by water on three sides. The proximity and intensity of the sea here probably figured heavily in Joyce's choice of water as the dominant symbol in Chapter One, and it reverberates throughout the

"It was cold and dark under the seawall beside his father's house." Martello Terrace, Bray and the seawall. Joyce's house is number one, next to the boathouse. The Vances lived at number 4.

11

book.

The strand in front of the house is broad and cheerful. On the west side the high ground supports a Martello tower and a string of villas which combine with the sea and the gulls to give a heightened holiday feeling, an openness and airyness which contrast sharply with the dampness of Clongowes and, later, with the gloom of the city. The exhilaration and good humour at the beginning of the Christmas dinner are consistant with the setting in which Simon Dedalus and Mr Casey enjoyed their morning walk.

The Royal Marine Hotel where Stephen stood with Eileen Vance looking into the sunny ground is located on the corner of Quinsborough Road, within sight of Joyce's house. Though the grounds are small, little more than a terrace, the gardens of the adjoining houses and a secluded lane beside the railway tracks combine to make them pleasant. Stanislaus Joyce remembers the level crossing next to the hotel in *My Brother's Keeper* and details the route down Quinsborough to the griffin-topped fountain in front of the town hall on the south end of Main Street, taken by William O'Connell (Uncle Charles) as he did the shopping for Mrs Joyce. It is actually a much longer walk than Stanislaus implies, though short enough to a man who later covered 'ten or twelve miles of the road' on a Sunday ramble. Quinsborough Road is lined with some imposing residences recalling that Dublin's biggest railway magnate went into bankruptcy trying to turn Bray into the Brighton of Ireland earlier in the century. In fact the houses on the north side of the street very strongly reflected that oriental look associated with Brighton. Seapoint Road, parallel to Quinsborough, but following the course of the Bray river from Main Street to Martello Terrace, was also frequented by the Joyces, Stanislaus recalling that the two boys rode its length on a donkey.

John Joyce and James Vance, whose family lived at number 4 in the terrace, were good friends and their children James and Eileen were inseparable though the Joyce children's governess, 'Dante' Conway, disapproved because the Vances were Protestants (descended from a Huguenot family named Vans). Stanislaus Joyce remembered Mr Vance as a cheerful, hard-working man, but his wife was a semi-invalid who suffered from heart disease and died when relatively young. Vance kept chemist's shops with his brother William in Main Street and on little Albert Walk near the strand where James was apparently treated after being bitten by a dog (he remained frightened of dogs throughout his life and ascribed this characteristic to Stephen).

One feature of the friendship between James and Eileen may have included exchanging poems as the echo of a few lines of Eileen's noted in the endpaper of her copy of the *Arabian Nights*, turns up in *A Portrait*. Fleming had written, 'for a cod', in Stephen's geography:

> Stephen Dedalus is my name,
> Ireland is my nation.

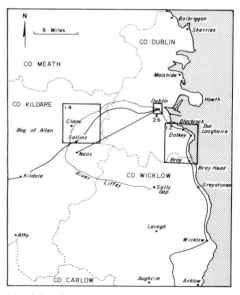

Map 1.1. *A Portrait: the broad view.*

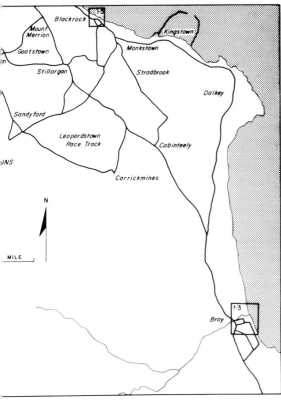

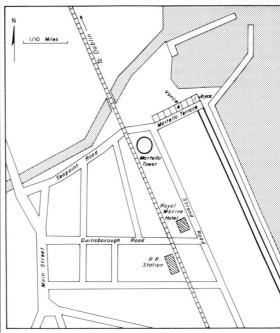

Map 1.3. Martello Terrace, Bray.

Map 1.2. Blackrock and Bray.

"Yes . . . O, well now, we got a good breath of ozone round the Head today" — Simon Dedalus.
Bray Esplanade and Bray Head from Martello Terrace. (Lawrence Collection, NL1)

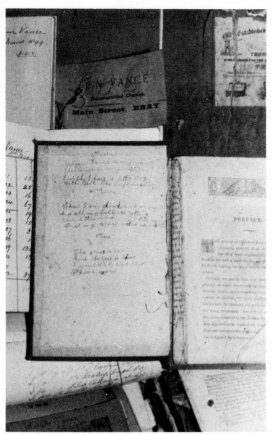

'When I am dead and in my grave . . . This little book will tell my name'. The inscription in Eileen Vance's *Arabian Nights*.

Clongowes is my dwellingplace
And heaven my expectation.

Eileen's three verses had begun:

Eileen Vance is my name,
Ireland is my nation.
I wish I had a little dog
With tail like inflammation.

Not an elegant effort, but in keeping with the sort of jocular, casual entertainment that went on between the two families.

The Christmas dinner is clearly set at the house in Bray, but the actual incident deviates from the sequence of events suggested in *A Portrait* in that it took place in December 1891, after Parnell's death (October 1891) and after Joyce

had left Clongowes. With the death so recent, the argument between the elder Dedalus and Mr Casey on the one side and Dante on the other is fiercer than it might otherwise have been. John Joyce and John Kelly (the model for Casey) were long-time partisans of Parnell ('My dead king', Casey cries), and their loyalty only intensified after he was 'betrayed' by the clergy and abandoned by the Irish Parliamentary Party. In *A Portrait* Casey mentions a political meeting in Arklow, south of Bray in County Wicklow, where he supported Parnell in the face of his detractors. Joyce's use of Arklow as the scene of Casey's 'very famous spit' recalls that Parnell was born near Arklow in Avondale House, which is close to the Meeting of the Waters in the Vale of Avoca. In the midst of the pathos and venom of the Christmas dinner Joyce interjects his own brand of ironic humour by having Casey's spit and Dante's spit collide over the table in a similar meeting of the waters.

Kelly had also been very active in support of Michael Davitt's Land League and had suffered imprisonment and a permanently crippled hand, the result of forced labour during several periods of confinement. Davitt was also Dante's other hero, but it was he who cast the first important vote against Parnell when the scandal surrounding his relationship with Mrs O'Shea became too much for the politicians, betraying the confidence of 'the Chief' and Casey/Kelly as well. Davitt's treachery, echoed by Dante, the self-serving outrage displayed by churchmen (including 'Billy with the lip' and 'the tub of guts up in Armagh' — Archbishop Walsh and Cardinal Logue) and the volte-face of the rabblement fostered Joyce's later attachment to the idea of betrayal and coincided with John Joyce's own downhill slide and his conviction that he, too, was the victim of a conspiracy.

Despite the discomfort and then terror which the scene at the dinner table induces in Stephen, he clearly associates his early childhood at Martello Terrace with warmth and affection, comparing his memories of home with Clongowes to the school's disadvantage. By all accounts the house at Bray was a hospitable and often rollicking place, filled with the voices of John Joyce and his cronies or with the sounds of Mrs Joyce accompanying singers at the piano. It is little wonder then that the boy was so deeply affected by the family's rapid descent into impecuniosity and the consequent changes in all their lives.

Clongowes Wood College (pp. 8-27; 40-59)

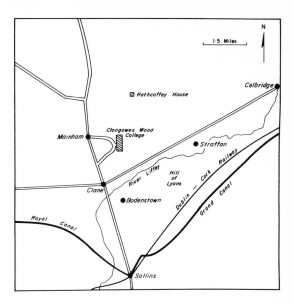

Map 1.4. Clongowes Wood College.

The picture of Clongowes Wood College drawn in *A Portrait* suits Joyce's purpose in the novel but is not otherwise an entirely accurate account of his experience there. Compared to many contemporary institutions, it was a remarkably humane and enlightened establishment. The feeling of confinement and regimentation suggested by Stephen's grim plodding through halls, up and down stairs, and from one activity to another is nevertheless reflected in the schedule set for the boys; this included early rising, prayers, Mass and study before breakfast, classes throughout the forenoon, recreation and more study before dinner, recreation, a visit to the Blessed Sacrament and more studies before supper, and then recreation and prayers before bed. The school was also a large one, magnified by Stephen's own size and youth.

The castle, the principal building at Clongowes, had some stimulating associations for the boy. It had been Castle Browne, property of the family of the 'Marshall' killed at Prague in 1757, and earlier of the Eustace family, Anglo-Normans who forfeited the property during the Cromwellian Settlement because of their Roman Catholic faith and their

activities on behalf of the Irish in the 1641 Rising. Both this structure and the neighbouring one at Rathcoffey were razed by Cromwell's soldiers. To these hints of heroism and martyrdom was added the famous incident involving Hamilton Rowan, the United Irishman, who had built a house about two miles through the woods from Clongowes on the ruins of old Rathcoffey Castle. This story was quite possibly apocryphal — Rowan is said to have been out of the country at the time — but it was current among the boys in Joyce's day. Rowan was believed to have escaped arrest at Rathcoffey during the events of the 1798 Rising (the opening episode of this rebellion took place near Clane) by fleeing to Castle Browne where, throwing his hat from the library window to deceive his pursuers (leading them to believe he had passed through the castle and out the back), he hid in the north-east tower chamber behind a door disguised as a bookcase. The hall door gave evidence that shots had been fired at the nimble Rowan. The hall and the round room were remnants of the original castle and had been preserved by Thomas Browne who purchased

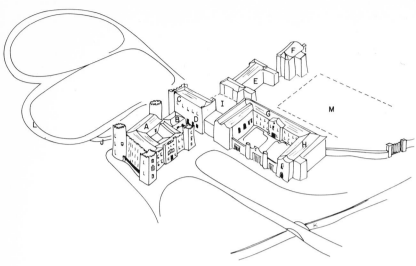

Figure 1: Clongowes Wood College, c. 1888-1891.

A. Castle — Community's quarters
   Rector's Office — 1st floor front
B. Kitchens — also "long corridor" whi
   curved along from the landing abo
   the refectory to the first floor of t
   castle.
C. Upstairs — Study Hall
D. Downstairs — Refectory
E. "Little boys' house" — recreation
   room — this building has been exte
   sively rebuilt. The pool is between th
   structure and the refectory.
F. Infirmary (James Joyce lived on th
   first floor).
G. Higher Line Boys — Dormitories a
   study rooms.
H. "People's" and Boys' Chapel. A ne
   chapel, not shown in this sketch, too
   the place of the wall and gate in t
   higher line quadrangle. The buildi
   marked 'G' and the one adjoining a
   also gone.
I. Intermediate corridor connecting t
   little boys' house to the refectory
   the "long corridor" pictured in t
   Ellman biography of Joyce. Th
   section closest to the refectory h
   been rebuilt.
J. "Ha-ha" where Hamilton Rowen w
   said to have thrown his hat to ma
   his pursuers believe he had escap
   over the fields behind the castle.
K. 'Nellie's ditch' — the "square ditc
   of *A Portrait*
L. Cinder track
M. Bakery, laundries, kitchen gardens
   previously a stable area.

The Square (Nellie's) Ditch. Wells shoulders Stephen into the square ditch in front of the castle.

The People's Chapel at Clongowes. On Sundays, the people of Clane worshipped here.

the house from its Cromwellian beneficiary, Sir Richard Reynall, in 1667.

The grounds of Rathcoffey were visible from Clongowes and often served for recreational outings for the boys. The estate was graced by magnificent beech trees and a feeling of romance and adventure altogether so attractive that the walk there constituted a favourite form of exercise. The grounds of the college also revealed two sections of the old Pale wall, one on either side of the castle (northeast and southwest) and each about five or ten minutes distant by foot. Clongowes had been one of the castle outposts of the Pale, which had guarded the Anglo-Normans from the forays of the natives.

These features and the bucolic estates and other historic and mythical attributes of the landscape combined to give the setting a charm which is not apparent in *A Portrait*. More engaging to the child's mind was the 'square ditch', the so-called 'Nellie's ditch'. Half drain, half the result of an architectural ideal known as the 'moated grange', it had been the scene of the drowning of a laundrymaid sometime previously. The still, brown water in the ditch was duplicated indoors by the waters of the bathing pool built just before Joyce entered the school and filled, until recently, with bog water. The pool is located between the little boys' dormitories and the refectory, so it must have been very frequently thrust into the boy's consciousness. The presence of the intensely sombre graveyard 'off the main avenue of limes' may also have exerted a sobering influence. Several students of the college have indeed been buried in this dark and silent recess, collected in rows near the slumbering bones of members of the community.

The Joyces came to Clongowes by way of the G. S. & W. Railroad to Sallins, a pretty canal village. They then travelled north by coach through the ancient village of Clane, past the turn-off to Bodenstown,

the burial place of Wolfe Tone, and across the gentle landscape to the entrance to the castle grounds. Near the entrance is a castellated gate (the 'Grand gate') which gives on to the avenue of limes and the little graveyard of which Stephen speaks. The castle lies in the dim distance, beyond the bridge over Nellie's ditch. To the right of the castle, where the new chapel (1906) now stands, there was a quadrangle which housed the older dormitories, playrooms and classrooms, and the higher line library, as well as the People's Chapel, attended by the boys of the school and the residents of Clane. This group of buildings was enclosed by its own gate built in the same style, though not as elaborately, as the entrance gate. These buildings, as well as the infirmary and the refectory/study hall, were added between 1819 and 1874, the refectory rebuilt in 1897 after a fire. Only the People's Chapel now remains of the quadrangle, but it has been shortened by some fifteen feet at the altar end to accommodate new classrooms. Joyce portrays it in all the dank and gloom that the Irish climate, early nightfalls and stone walls can muster, but it is actually extremely bright and lovely, a product of the baroque infatuation with light. The foreshortening has left it unbalanced, heavily dominated by the altar, but this was not so in Joyce's time and the cream and brown of the walls and pillars and the reds and golds of the altar are warm and inviting.

Behind and to the right of the chapel, bakeries and laundries and other domestic props to the institution occupied the area formerly given over to stables. The water enclosed by the square ditch flows past the edge of the outbuildings which are also enclosed by a gate.

The sense of distance between places in the school is pronounced in *A Portrait* and this is only partially due to the fact that the whole is being paced by a little boy. Apart from the higher line buildings and the chapel, the college is laid out in a line with the castle at one end and the infirmary at the other; the kitchens, refectory and study-hall, and other classrooms and dormitories lie in between. Ordinarily the boys would not have spent a great deal of time at the castle, which was taken up entirely by the community. James, however, was a favourite and in some respects a ward of the rector, John Conmee, and was frequently to be found sprawled in front of the fire in his office (from time to time other boys also enjoyed this privilege) which was on the first floor, to the left of the large front windows in the castle hall. It was a long walk from there to the little boys' quarters and further still to the infirmary where Joyce, because of his age, actually lived for much of his time at Clongowes, under the care of the nurse, Nanny Galvin, and the infirmarian, Brother Hanly. His bedroom was on the first floor, above the treatment rooms.

The illness which strikes Stephen at Clongowes may actually have taken place, though probably later, as records show that a doctor called in to treat Joyce towards the end of his third year at the school. This raises the question of time as it relates both to the novel and to Joyce's own life. The first segment about Clongowes in *A Portrait* quite definitely takes place during Stephen's first year, since it is clear that he has not had his first Christmas holiday (1888). Yet the events surrounding the death of Parnell which are associated with his illness did not occur until October 1891. This confuses the notion that these events are part of Joyce's actual recollection, though it does not affect his use of the fond and familiar Brother Hanly as the sorrowing Brother Michael, or other elements of the infirmary routine. Joyce himself attended Clongowes between the autumn of 1888 and sometime in 1891. There is some difference of opinion as to when he actually left the institution, but since his father was not billed for any expenses accrued during autumn of 1891,

it seems safe to assume that Joyce did not come back to school after the summer holidays. Various reasons are given for this state of affairs, all associated with the elder Joyce's declining fortunes. In any case, it is wiser to look at these episodes through the sensitive and impressionable mind of the boy Stephen than from a biographical point of view.

Likewise, the pandying incident may or may not have taken place — there is no record to document much of Joyce's daily life at Clongowes — but it is interesting to plot Stephen's movements to see where Joyce deviates from reality in the interest of effect here as well as elsewhere. The corridor into which Stephen ventures in the aftermath of the pandying episode is between the castle and the refectory. He speaks of the boys leaving after dinner according to 'line'. This segregation by age was a principal aspect of Clongowes, extending to the provision of separate work and play areas, and in the dining hall, separate tables. Joyce effectively uses it to isolate Stephen and prolong events. Beyond the refectory door he turns to his right and ascends the stairs to the landing (a second flight rises parallel to the first and leads to the study hall). The stair hall is square and lofty and has a gothic look about it which may well have contributed to the intensity of Stephen's feelings. At the landing he enters the 'low dark corridor that led to the castle'. This is not the corridor usually pictured above the caption 'the long walk' or 'the long corridor', which was the hallway between the refectory and the little boy's establishment. Rather, it curves away from the landing to the left, entering the castle hall through an intervening room at the back, diagonally across the stair well from the rector's office. It is not such a long walk, and was quite emphatically not a frightening one for young Joyce — recalling that he had spent many contented hours with Fr Conmee. The feeling that the boy is impelled down a long broad straight hall to the foot of the rector's door, like a victim to the scaffold, is not borne out by the actual setting, in which there are several corners for the boy to pause and reflect and perhaps turn back. The portraits, however, are there, and it is dark and silent, tucked as it is above the kitchens behind a masking wall. Interestingly he includes the figure of the servant outside the ironing room on the landing in the main hall. This same room featured prominently in the legend concerning the appearance of the bloodied marshall in the castle at the hour of his death in far-off Prague; the servants who witnessed his corporeal return were gathered here. The fact that the marshall died in Prague rather played into the hands of Joyce the ironist. In the kind of coincidence which delighted him, and which often constituted the creative impetus he required, Prague happened to be the favourite city of John Conmee, who loved all things graced by the patina of age and was a romantic at heart. This fact combined with the heroism of the marshall's story lends a great deal of dash to the determined little figure and helps explain his kindly reception in the rector's office.

Fr Dolan, about whom Stephen meant to complain, was the prefect, Fr Daly. Joyce himself tells us this in the events surrounding the purchase of the turkey for Christmas dinner. 'That's the real ally-daly', the shop assistant asserts — and Stephen's thoughts immediately turn to the pandybat, also called a 'turkey'. There is no reason to believe that Daly actually meted out the punishment — this responsibility may have been assigned to 'Mr Barrett' — but one other detail concerning the prefect rings true. Daly came to Clongowes to assist Fr Conmee in his efforts to reorganize the school after its amalgamation with Tullabeg. While Clongowes was reputed to be the finest school in Ireland, Tullabeg actually had a higher academic standard. It was Daly's mission to sharpen

indolent minds among Clongowians and bring them up to Tullabeg's level. He was said to have been a perfect martinet in the service of his goal and might well have frequently lectured the boys about that bankrupt but formidable institution. His attitude also may have led Joyce to mark him for the pandier.

Directly behind the castle a lawn rises above the ha-ha, and the track and playing fields stretch away to the surrounding woods. Games and other recreation formed an important part of school life and the boys frequently took long walks, kindly shepherded or vigourously marched depending upon the master involved. Joyce, being so young, did not join in much of this activity until his third year, when he moved into the little boys' facilities and began the regular course of schooling. But from the first he was subject to the pre-eminently spiritual atmosphere and there is every reason to believe that the violence of Stephen's rejection of the church can be at least partially explained by the intensity of his early adherence. (Joyce later declared that the Jesuits bred athiests.) In this regard it may be worthwhile to note Joyce's life-long prediliction for word play and how it may be brought to bear here. Jokes involving Irish place-names were standard in linguistic humour and prior to his authorship of *A Portrait* Joyce is known to have thoroughly examined P.W. Joyce's *Irish Names of Places*. Stephen takes part in this kind of game with Athy in the infirmary, trying to respond to the riddle, 'Why is the county Kildare like the leg of a fellow's breeches?' If he could have forseen the future he might well have varied this exceedingly variable question by asking 'Why is the county Kildare like Stephen Dedalus?' For in the etymology of the name Kildare, *Kil* = church. They both had an apostate in them.

Blackrock (pp. 60-65)

Early in 1892 the Joyce family moved to Blackrock. John Joyce was experiencing financial difficulties, but the sale of some of his property in Cork allowed them to take a very substantial house at 23 Carysfort Avenue. The summer spent there, the last before the move into the city centre, became the basis for the first part of Chapter Two in *A Portrait*. Though many of the actuating elements in Chapter One reappear in this section — the cinder track at Clongowes has its echo in the circular track in the park, the organized activities of his school days are reflected in the repetitive and often circular excursions of the summer, the constricted pose of the sailor's hornpipe has its analogue in the running technique favoured by Mike Flynn — as the chapter progresses, Stephen grows dissatisfied with movement which is prescribed and strikes out in a tentative exploration of life, alone, at night, and in a psychological sense, entirely on his own.

Blackrock became a fashionable suburb in the eighteenth century, and after a period of decline — brought about by the construction of the Kingstown and Bray branch of the Dublin and Southeast Railroad which, in turn, provoked the formation of a very disagreeable salt marsh — became, with civic improvement, a prosperous suburb. The town was established very early as a place of resort as it marked the farthest extent visited by the Lord Mayor and his entourage in their procession around the Liberties and franchises of the Dublin corporation, a rite discontinued only a few years before the Joyces moved to Blackrock. Carysfort Avenue lay just outside the old corporation boundary; therefore, when the inevitable move to Dublin comes, crossing the line has both historical and deep personal significance for Stephen and artistic value for Joyce. One other topographical aspect of the area contributes in this framework. The Joyce house lay just below a little eminence called 'Eagle Hill'. Recalling Joyce's depiction of Parnell as a fallen eagle, and Stephen's downcast fate, his association with Parnell and his move from the environs of the hill carries the same kind of symbolic import.

Number 23 Carysfort Avenue, called 'Leoville' and ornamented by a stone lion recumbent over the porch (the old National University on Stephen's Green has the same kind of lion embellishment), now occupies the corner of Carysfort Avenue and Frescati Road, though when the Joyces lived there Frescati Road did not exist and another house and a path running through to George's Place separated their house from Christ Church and its gardens. This whole area is much changed. Christ Church is gone and Frescati Road cuts through what was the Fitzwilliam estate on the north side of George's Avenue. This broad, spare boulevard belies the earlier existence of several lovely estates between Merrion Avenue and Rock Hill.

Every day Uncle Charles and Stephen followed the same itinerary: down the avenue to one or two of the numerous shops in Main Street, along Rock Hill to the gate and down the gorge into the People's Park where Stephen ran the track under the failing eye of Mike Flynn while the latter leaned against the railway gate at the south-east corner. While Flynn and Uncle Charles sat beside the bandstand, Stephen had time to question his father's estimation of the old trainer, as he did later the object of his granduncle's piety when they visited St John the Baptist's Church on Newtown Avenue before returning home. Joyce, of course, does not mention that the chapel is St John's, but we recognize it as the kind of touch Joyce was fond of, remembering the method by which his uncle helped the boy to holy water.

The boy's second routine excursion took

Main Street, Blackrock. At one end Rock Hill, at the
other the Cross which had marked the old Corporation
boundary. (Lawrence Collection, NLI).

Map 1.5. Blackrock. Key: (a) 23 Carysfort Avenue,
Joyce Residence (1892). (b) Rock Hill gate. (c) Gate
near railway station. (d) Bandstand, Blackrock Park.
(e) St. John the Baptist Catholic Church. (f) 'Castle'
— ornamental embattled structure above the rocks
where the 'gang of adventurers' fought battles. (g) Christ
Church.

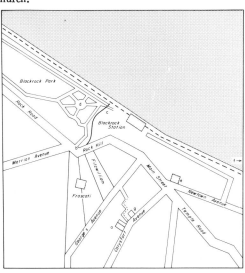

'The house in Carysfort Avenue' — 'Leoville' number 23.

place on Sundays when Stephen, his father, and Uncle Charles took a long walk. This was a popular kind of outing at the time, and the scene has a certain avuncular humour about it in the beginning, but it fades as Joyce relates that the two older men habitually used the occasion to re-explore outmoded themes in politics and family legend in 'grimy wayside public-houses' rather than the exceptionally beautiful countryside. Their routes them-selves reflect the tedium which these holi-days came to represent to Stephen. The two routes, left from Stillorgan towards the Dublin Mountains, or straight by the Goatstown Road to Dundrum, coming home by way of Sandyford, may well have beem one and the same, the first circling clockwise, the second, anticlockwise. If not, the first of the routes would have traced the familiar way to Carrickmines.

Chapter Two brings into focus the increasingly Byronesque Stephen, who alternately braved it with his band of adventures on the jagged rocks along the shore behind Blackrock House or succumbed to spells of solitary reverie centred on the figure of Mercedes. His environment provided ample encourage-ment for both moods. In the previous century Rock Road was heavily frequent-ed by highwaymen and several spirited engagements followed the formation of vigilance committees; the reefs behind Blackrock House, surmounted by an ornamental embattled structure, were the scene of a famous shipping disaster, the wreck of the *Prince of Wales,* in 1807; Frescati, across George's Avenue from the Joyce's back garden, was the favour-ite home of the martyred patriot, Lord Edward Fitzgerald, and was searched by authorities seeking his arrest. South and west of the town were numerous picturesque reminders of the redoubtable past. In addition, the physical landscape was a harmonious instrument with which to play.

With the coming of autumn Stephen becomes more confined and at the same time more introverted. His sphere is limited to the avenue and the milk route which seems to have conformed to the route of the tram-tracks between Rock Hill and Temple Hill before it terminated at Strad-brook. These restrictions are symptomatic of the succeeding episodes where, though Stephen is free to move about the city, he is painfully aware of numerous social and spiritual constraints. It is important for the reader to understand that the boy's physical surroundings undergo a drastic change. Nowhere south of the city was as built up as it now appears. The environs of Stillorgan, for example, were still largely in the hands of estate-owners, and a Sunday jaunter could walk for miles without meeting any obstacle more formidable than a stile. Such commercial centres as Dublin and Kingstown (Dun Laoghaire) had been the scene of visits (Stephen has obviously seen the pier at Kingstown and the Wicklow Hotel as well as the route to the Kingsbridge Station in Dublin), but his life had been conducted within the more congenial boundaries of Bray, Blackrock and Clongowes. The poor, in Stephen's frame of reference, inhabited such dwellings as the little cottages in Clane: holy peasants in holy cottages — perhaps like the one in which Stephen imagines Mercedes lives, or like the cottage just outside of Sandyford whose entry-way was inscribed with the motto: 'Content in a Cottage, and Envy to no One'. The 'bare cheerless house' in Fitzgibbon Street provides an unpleasant introduction to a degraded future.

Chapter Two

THE GLOOMY FOGGY CITY

The Bare Cheerless House (pp. 65-72)

Stephen and his mother board the train at Blackrock Station on their way to the city, and as they travel north, they prophetically watch their household furnishings moving away from them along the Merrion Road. Though their goods probably all arrived intact after this move, they did not all survive subsequent removals, lost as the years and addresses went by to attrition and the pawnshops. The house the Joyces moved to, after a short stay on Hardwicke Street, was at 14 Fitzgibbon Street, the last of their fashionable residences, although even then it was a decided move down the social scale from Blackrock. The neighbouring Mountjoy Square had visibly declined since its hey-day, and Gardiner Street, once the pride of Georgian Dublin, had become so many tenements. Like John Joyce, Dublin was intensely conscious of its glorious past. It had lost its place as a spirited if not formidable capital of Europe after the Act of Union in 1800, thereby losing a large number of its most distinguished residents and their lively society. As a result, it had fallen, especially on the north side of the Liffey, from splendor through a sort of desperate shabby gentility to dereliction, and as a city it was only too aware of it. On a visit to the city in 1882 George Moore felt compelled to describe the 'brawling, ignorance and plaintive decay' which surrounded him and concluded that the 'souls of the Dubliners blend and harmonize with their connatural surroundings'. Joyce described it as paralysis — inanition — and gives the impression that what the inhabitants lacked in substance they made up for with inane attempts at amusement, braggadocio, meanness, ineffectual grieving, and visits to the sacraments. His overall impression is characterized by almost unmitigated gloom.

The city was small in area and therefore completely accessible to the pedestrian, and Joyce, fond of long walks, took full advantage of its streets. The Liffey, an open sewer until 1906, served as the border between the tradesman's, the cleric's, the navvy's north and the cultural, professional ambience of the south (though the slums in the environs of the Castle were intolerably bad). Joyce had been born a 'southsider', and his family's move into the north of the city was conspicuous evidence of the decline in their fortunes. In 1890, half the city's population of 250,000 lived in slums, the worst of which lay between Fitzgibbon Street and the River Liffey, directly in Stephen's path as he walked to the quays or into the nororious prostitute district which was centred on Mabbot (Corporation) Street, Montgomery (Foley) Street, and Tyrone (Railway) Street. Another visitor to Dublin in the eighties remarked on the number of young people wandering the streets. In fact, many such children, who had not found homes by way of prostitution or charity, simply lived in the streets, begging. Drunkenness was endemic and as four-fifths of the population were working class or lower, very little attention was paid to poverty.

Joyce construes Stephen's adjustment to his new circumstances as slow and painful. Along with his father's 'betrayal' and his Uncle Charles' senility, the gloomy, smoke-shrouded labyrinth of the city was 'a new complex sensation'. At first Stephen is only bold enough to circle around Mountjoy Square in movement reminiscent of the Blackrock episodes, but when he had mapped out the city in his mind (Stephen and Joyce had this inclination in common), he took one of its main arteries, Gardiner Street Lower, to the Custom House which fronts on the Liffey at Custom House Quay. During the course of his years in Dublin, it is certain that Joyce fully explored the docks and quays along the North Wall: the Old, Inner, and George's Docks; the railroad termini lined up along the wall to receive the bulk of merchandise handled by the port of Dublin; the sheds, stores, and wharves belonging to the steam packet companies; the graving dock, Customs Watch House and all the other facilities on the North Wall extension. The area was a hive of activity and swarmed with porters, agents, and provisioners, the quay police whose odd uniforms and beards distinguished them from the regular city police and made them seem ill-dressed to Stephen, passengers from the steam packets and for the cross-river ferries, and no doubt prostitutes, who, like their better-off sisters who left their cards in officers' messes and personally welcomed distinguished visitors to Horse Show Week and other festivities, plied their trade among the newly arrived sailors from their houses in the neighbouring streets to the north. Characteristically, he tries to imagine himself in Marseilles. Both his impressions of that city and the qualities associated with Mercedes are drawn from his reading in *The Count of Monte Cristo* during his hiatus from school in Blackrock. Stephen's version is at slight variance with Dumas's, but the relationship between the contrite Mercedes (another 'Mary', this time from the Spanish 'Mary of Mercies'), and the magnanimous Edmond Dantes is one with which he is entirely sympathetic.

Several of Joyce's mother's relatives lived in the city, among them Mrs Lyons and Mrs Callanan, and Mrs Callanan's daughter Mary Ellen, Joyce's great-aunts

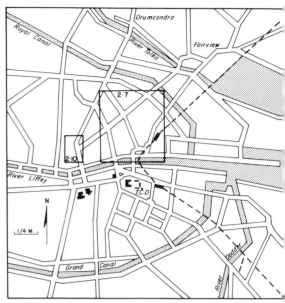

Map 2.6. Showing location for Maps 2.7 (North of the Liffey) and 2.10 (Church Street) below.

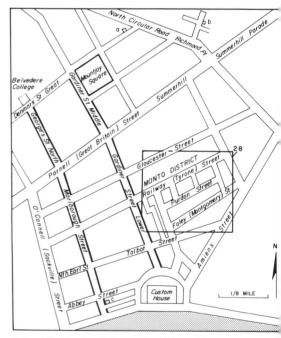

Map 2.7. North of the Liffey. (a) 14 Fitzgibbon Street, Joyce residence (1893); (b) 17 Richmond Street, Joyce residence (1894-97); (c) Morgue.

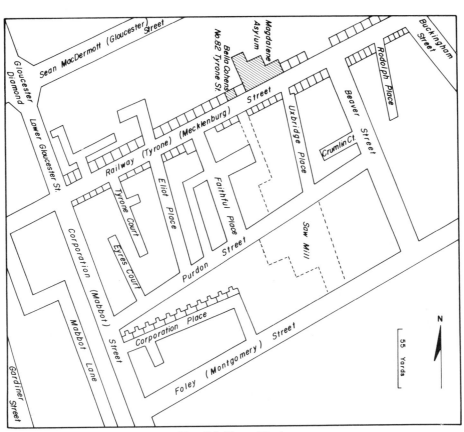

Map. 2.8. Monto District.

'In the beginning he contented himself with circling timidly round the neighbouring square'. Mountjoy Square.

and cousin respectively, who kept the Misses Flynn school at 15 Usher's Island. This house, described in detail in 'The Dead', is the location of the 'narrow breakfastroom high up in the old dark-windowed house' where, in *A Portrait*, a senile old woman, one of the aunts, confuses Stephen with 'Josephine' (Mary Ellen). The ground floor was and still is occupied by a seed merchant, and the quay was lined with commercial establishments and tenements, but the house was a respectable one and provided the scene for many Christmas parties and other get-togethers throughout Joyce's childhood. Mrs Joyce's sister-in-law, Josephine Murray, also lived in the city at various addresses around the North Strand Road area and south of the Liffey around Shelbourne Road, and her home is the probable setting for the other short kitchen episode in Chapter Two, especially since James took an interest in his cousin Katsy Murray, the ringletted girl in *A Portrait* who exhibits one of the traits Joyce ascribes to women — namely guile.

During this early period Stephen also attends a party in Harold's Cross, riding home afterwards on a tram with E--C--. He sets the party at Harold's Cross in order to make the long tram-ride home possible for both of them and, tangentially, because the area was one which he could associate with the Mercedes-drama. The green at Harold's Cross remained very rustic until 1894, just after the time during which the party is supposed to have taken place, and looked southwards upon open country and the mountains. In addition, and more important to the symbolic framework of the novel, it had been the scene of both enthusiastic Mayday celebrations and earlier, of hangings, being the site (St Patrick's) from which the Archbishop of Dublin dispensed corporal justice. The relationship between the designation 'Harold's Cross' and the narrative should not be overlooked: the Harolds were a

powerful branch of an Anglo-Norman family who held sway in this area for hundreds of years (Joyce's ancestry was also Anglo-Norman); 'Cross' refers to their seat — and Stephen looks like nothing so much as the haughty young scion at his restless ease — but also calls up the Cross which Christ suffered, with reference to the Archbishop's gallows and E--C--'s cowled head. The strands of this fabric are dense: E--C--, her antecedents: the pagan temptress of the Mayday rite, Mercedes, the Blessed Virgin, the Virgin Mother, Joyce's mother (who often accompanied him to parties, including those at the Sheehey's upon which this episode appears to be based in spirit, if not in fact) — all are integrated with the symbolic character of this setting.

One further detail should be noted. Joyce was quite familiar with this neighbourhood and the way home because his grandfather and step-grandmother lived at 7 Clanbrassil Street, a few steps north of the Grand Canal and Harold's Cross Road. Clanbrassil Street is one of the four areas directly or indirectly referred to in *A Portrait* which have Jewish overtones: a feature which partially informs Stephen's status as a 'dispossessed son'. Another of the areas is John Joyce's boyhood neighbourhood, South Terrace, Cork, which included a synagogue and Hebrew school. Fairview Strand/Philipsburgh Avenue, Richmond Avenue, the former the location of the old Jewish burying ground and mortuary chapel, the latter of homes belonging to members of the Jewish colony, were recognizably Jewish in character owing, in the latter case, to the custom which dictated that their doors must not face the street (Joyce's house on Richmond Avenue faced an inner courtyard). The fourth locality so designated is that surrounding Davin's room on Grantham Street. Stephen is quite familiar with this area, mentioning it twice with regard to Davin and once in relation to Cranly, whom he meets at the Harcourt Street station. The theme of the 'wandering Jew' has obvious appeal for Stephen, but aside from this, Judaism seems to incorporate a certain ingenuousness which comes to attract him wherever he encounters it. Walking with Davin one evening he is aware that he is in the 'dark narrow streets of the poorer Jews' (Pleasant Street, Lombard Street) and it is here that Davin confides the story of his chance meeting with the young woman in the cottage. The woman in the story is spoken of as being unpractised in guile and is compared with the gentle women of Clane and Stephen himself — both 'batlike soul[s] waking to the consciousness of [themselves] in darkness and secrecy and loneliness. . .'. Earlier, wandering through Monto's dingy laneways, he wondered if he had 'strayed into the quarter of the Jews', and follows with an image depicting a pagan rite. Both images, one tender, one obscene, have a natural quality: they are spiritually and temporally uncultivated. This becomes an underlying feature of Stephen's new religion of art.

A Portrait is equivocal with regard to the exact address of Stephen's 'bare cheerless house' in the city. In reality, the Joyces moved to 14 Fitzgibbon Street where they remained a year, went to 2 Millbourne Lane in Drumcondra, staying about ten months, and then moved back to the vicinity of Fitzgibbon, to 17 North Richmond Street, when this house, owned by John Joyce, became vacant. After remaining on this dead-end street for four years, they moved to Fairview, outside the city proper. In the novel, Joyce elects to keep Stephen within the city, apparently at 14 Fitzgibbon, until sometime after the confession scene, and to use the Drumcondra address out of its actual order, placing it just before the family's move to Fairview. This change is central to the symbolic movement of the book. It did not suit Joyce's purposes to have Stephen escape too soon from the congestion and gloom of the city, and as long as he lived on or near Fitzgibbon Street, he had him symbolically entrapped by the double circles of water formed by the rivers and canals of Dublin. The force and meaning of the move to Fairview, then, becomes clear when Joyce reveals it just as Stephen is rejecting the life of the Church; at this point he has grown emotionally beyond the bounds of the city and is ready for his move east to the sea. The topographical structure of the novel also allows Joyce to balance the movement out of the city with the earlier trip from Blackrock to the city, achieving a symmetry in the movement and bringing the oppressive atmosphere of Dublin to bear on the middle phases of Stephen's development without relief. Additional tactical advantage is gained as Joyce is able to detain Stephen in close proximity to the prostitute district and is later able to send him directly west to the Capuchin Church in Church Street (opposed and balanced in the following chapter by the eastward journey to Bull Island).

This change, however, created one problem for Joyce. Stanislaus Joyce tells us that the episode in which Stephen is set upon by Heron, Boland and Nash for his defence of Byron, the excommunicated, disowned and exiled poet, really happened to his brother. At the time, the Joyces were living in Millbourne Lane, and some of Joyce's classmates overtook him on his way home from school on the Drumcondra Road. It was necessary to Joyce's technique to keep the actual location of these childhood incidents true-to-life; the physical details of place helped him to recreate the events and feelings they evoked. Joyce therefore places Stephen on Drumcondra Road 'with a letter'. Presumably he was on his way to the post office — there was one on Grattan Terrace — and his aunt and uncle John Murray lived nearby. The boys come along, and they all turn into Clonliffe Road for no ostensible reason, though we might imagine that they were headed towards the east-side city and suburban race and amusement grounds (now Croke Park and sports ground) which was off Jones Road. Joyce was fortunate in that this setting placed Stephen under the moral aegis of 'Buck' Jones and in the shadow of an earlier 'heroic stand'. Jones, a magistrate and resident at Clonliffe House (now superseded by the Archbishop's house and Holy Cross College), was beseiged there by a band of highwaymen during the course of his attempt to capture their leader, Larry Clinch. Jones honourably declined when Clinch's perfidious wife had offered to betray her husband and defeated him instead by force of arms. Unlike Stephen, he was assisted by a guard of the Tipperary Militia.

Belvedere College. After Whitsuntide play, Stephen co out onto the steps to see family waiting for him unde first lamp. Both the parlour w the director interviewed Ste and Joyce's English classr faced out to Great Den Street.

Figure 2. Belvedere College from the steps at back of Belvedere House c. 1906. At the left is the theatre/gymnasium; in the centre the chapel, classrooms and laboratories; on the right the shed where Stephen meets Heron and Wallis.

Belvedere College (pp. 73-86; 102-135)

In the spring of 1893 James Joyce entered Belvedere College. According to *A Portrait*, Simon Dedalus had accidently met Fr Conmee on a corner in Mountjoy Square, and in the course of conversation it was agreed that Stephen and his brother would be admitted to the school. With his fondness for connections and for being in the know, Dedalus had promoted Conmee to Provincial out of his time. The Jesuit had left Clongowes in 1891 to become Prefect of Studies at Belvedere. In 1892-93 he was teaching Latin and directing the school sodality. After two years as Prefect of Studies at University College and ten years as Prefect of the Jesuit house on Upper Gardiner Street (he would have been in residence there when Stephen passes after his talk with the director), he would become, in 1905, Provincial of the Jesuit Order in Ireland.

Joyce had been attending the Christian Brothers school on North Richmond Street during that spring but the family was not happy about it. Though Joyce does not place Stephen at the school, it is clearly a subject under discussion, Mrs Dedalus declaring that she 'never liked the idea of sending him to the christian brothers' and Stephen's father denouncing the place as suitable only for the likes of 'Paddy Stink' and 'Mickey Mud', an attitude which Joyce echoes in 'An Encounter' and hints at in *A Portrait*, though with less contempt, after his chance meeting with the four Brothers on Bull Wall. The Dedalus' are convinced of the superiority of a Jesuit education — Simon Dedalus for purely practical reasons — but the Brothers produced quite good results and the school was the *alma mater* of many famous men.

Stephen later notes his regard, even his affection for the Jesuits who taught him, and much is made of Joyce's expressed esteem for the priests of the order. Nevertheless, the evidence of his early notes for *A Portrait* and *Ulysses* (1903) as well as textual elements suggest that he also regarded them as not a little venial: supercilious, pandering, mincing unhealthily around the fringes of sexuality. The sticking-point ultimately lay elsewhere, however. Despite the relatively enlightened atmosphere of the Jesuit schools and Joyce's/Stephen's 'habit of quiet obedience', Stephen ultimately acted to throw off the close spiritual and intellectual guardianship imposed by his mentors at Belvedere, even though, as a dayschool, they could not exercise the same degree of supervision as was achieved at Clongowes.

Belvedere was a good school, a selective school, but also, unlike Clongowes, it was firmly ensconced in the middle and lower-middle class, by geographical situation, by population, by physical proportions. The institution on Great Denmark Street had been established in 1841 when Belvedere House was some seventy-five years old. The house was well-preserved and most of the original decoration had been restored a few years before Joyce entered the school. In the 1880s the Jesuits had expanded by incorporating the neighbouring town house at 5 Great Denmark Street and by constructing a gymnasium-theatre at the rear of number 5 and a new building along the back to house the boys' chapel, the science laboratories and additional classrooms. These new structures nearly engulfed the garden leaving a crabbed grassplot and a woebegone fountain, both of which have latterly been replaced by tarmacadam.

Dillon Cosgrave, writing in 1909, described the opulence of the main building:

> Belvedere House is the best preserved of the splendid old Dublin houses of the Georgian period. . . .The ornamentation by Lord Belvedere's Venetian artists was restored by the Jesuit Fathers a quarter of a century ago. The plaster reliefs on the walls and ceilings,

the Bossi marble chimney pieces, and the three rooms whose decoration was dedicated to Apollo, Venus and Diana respectively, are now in as good condition as they were a century ago. . .
> *(North Dublin*, p. 57).

Cosgrave was not accurate in attributing the decoration to Venetian artisans — the plasterwork was in fact done by a Dublin craftsman — nor with regard to the Venus ceiling, which was chastely replastered with flowers and geometric designs, but the building was a fine one. The stair hall, for example, was very gracefully laid out and highly ornamented. Yet it is so ill-lit that it seems as cramped and gloomy as Joyce's description of the city. The boys' dining-room and the parlour were on the first floor, and on the second, the community chapel and the three rooms dedicated to Venus, Diana and Apollo, which were used as classrooms.

Looking across the quadrangle from the steps at the rear of Belvedere House (see Fig. 2), the gymnasium-theatre was located on the left, built at right angles to the chapel and connected to it through the vestry. It was a single, large hall with two doors opening into the quadrangle, and its barrel-vaulted roof was fitted with glass panels through which the light streamed on the night of the Whitsuntide play. A stage with a draped proscenium had been built into one end and a simple balcony into the other. The walls were festooned with ranks of barbells and Indian clubs, reminding the audience that the building also served as the school's gymnasium: in fact, it was dedicated to this purpose in Joyce's penultimate year at Belvedere, amidst the usual flurry of rhetoric about strong young bodies — rhetoric infused in that age with a good measure of nationalist sentiment. These two facets of the patriotic Irishman combine later in *A Portrait* to emerge in the figure of Davin.

Occupying the ground floor of the new

three-storey building at the back of the quadrangle, the boys' chapel was a long, plain room with benches on either side of a central aisle. Windows lined both sides of the chapel: those on the south looked into the grass plot, those on the north into the back-gardens of the houses on Graham Court. As prefect of the Sodality of the Blessed Virgin during his last two years at Belvedere, Joyce, and Stephen, would have occupied a seat on one of the front benches before which was a slightly raised dais and a Victorian Gothic altarpiece, removed on the night of the Whitsuntide play to make room for the gymnasium equipment. The schoolroom where the rector announces the retreat was also on the ground floor and just to the right of the chapel. Stephen passes along the corridor outside this room to reach the shed where he meets Heron and Wallis on the night of the play. This shed formed the fourth side of the yard, opposite the theatre. Like the theatre, it has been replaced — with a more solid, but similar, structure.

In June 1895, the date which corresponds to Stephen's Whitsuntide play, Joyce had completed two full years at Belvedere. He had entered during the third trimester in 1893 in the third of grammar (which Stephen calls number six), and by 1895 was at the end of his junior year. He was not old enough to take the examinations for the middle grade, so in 1895-96 he enjoyed a hiatus during which he took private tuition, doing the middle and senior grades in the following two years. But even in 1895 Joyce was a recognized leader in the school having been elected secretary to the gymnasium (though not athletic and inclined to take sports more lightly than the sergeant-major would have wished) and chosen for the chief part in the play. He was not yet prefect of the sodality but his popularity, his scholastic merit and his piety marked him for that body 'chosen by vote of their companions and superiors,

and formed into an association for the purpose of showing special honour to the Virgin Mother of God' (*Belvederian*, p. 113). His execution of the obligations imposed upon members of the sodality was such that he was elected prefect in his middle year, which was unusually early, and re-elected for a second term in his senior year.

Among the characteristics assigned to Stephen Dedalus in early notes, Joyce declares that 'the applause following the fall of the curtain fired his blood more than the scene on the stage'; he felt the earth 'quaking'. In the heat of the moment he proceeds quickly from the stage, through the chapel, across the quadrangle, up the steps and into the hall which runs directly through the 'house' to the front. He sees

The chapel door, Belvedere College.

his family waiting for him under the first lamp on the pavement, but 'she' is not with them. Angry, he tells them that he has to leave a message in North Great George's Street and rushes off down the hill, coming to a halt finally in front of the morgue on Marlborough Street (now the site of the Abbey Theatre) which emerges into his consciousness as a concrete expression of his failed hopes. Fetid vapours reach him from the adjoining laneway, which even now retains the look of a mews. Significantly, he sees the word 'Lotts' on the walls, though this is Abbey Street Old, not Lotts Lane, which is on the other side of O'Connell Street. He may have reference to an establishment of that name in the alley or to the fact that after the area to the east was reclaimed from the Liffey, it was laid out and known by the name 'The Lots': if he does it is another of those coincidences Joyce was willing and able to make so much of. More likely, he associates the behaviour of E--C-- with the perversity of Lot's wife, juxtaposing 'pillar of gold' with the notion of the 'pillar of salt' in the welter of his experience with women.

Front entrance to Clongowes Wood Castle. Note its similarity to the Entrance at Queen's College, Cork (Lawrence Collection, NLI) shown over the next page.

Cork City (pp. 86-96)

In February 1894, just after Joyce's twelfth birthday and just before the family's move to Drumcondra, John Joyce and his son took the trip which is the basis for the Cork episode in *A Portrait*. The object of the trip was to dispose of the last of the elder Joyce's property in Cork: the holdings in the rear of South Terrace and those on Stable Lane had been sold the previous December; this time the remaining buildings at 7 and 8 Anglesea Street were to be sold — the money to be used to pay John Joyce's debts. This state of affairs is basic to an understanding of Stephen's frame of mind during this episode and contributes to Joyce's picture of Stephen as a disinherited son.

The atmosphere in Cork is quite different from that of Dublin, not because the real-life trip was an amiable change from home — though by all accounts both Joyces enjoyed themselves, staying in a first-class hotel on Pembroke Street, the Imperial, and making the old man's accustomed rounds — but because Joyce means to delineate as clearly as possible the dichotomy between Simon Dedalus's youth, a gilded youth, and Stephen's; to enhance the state of tension which exists between father and son with all the implicit loss of youth and innocence, of substance and grace, that chafes Stephen so cruelly and which binds him, however unwillingly, to his father.

Note that while Stephen's mind wanders

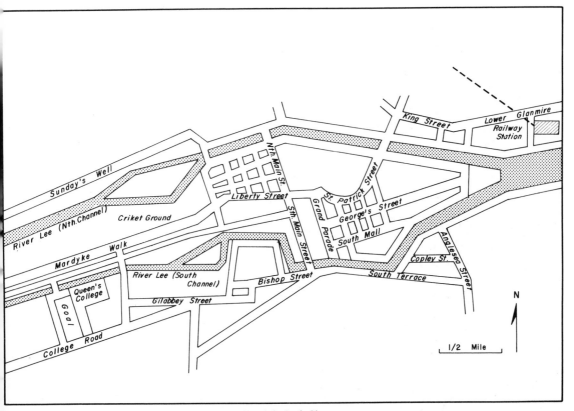

Map. 2.9. Cork City.

outside the limits of reality, or focuses on a view of reality unlike his father's, the city appears exactly as the elder Dedalus remembers. In keeping with his father's sentimentality, Joyce sets the scene in the summer, although the trip actually took place in the winter. Included as well are numerous examples of the kind of life his father lived which serve to animate the past and reinforce the poignancy of their situation: the 'Groceries' where Dedalus/Joyce and the same Harry Peard and little Jack Mountain, Bob Dyas and Maurice Moriarty, Tom O'Grady, Joey Corbet and Johnny Keevers of the Tantiles gathered after 'their names had been marked' on the class attendance list; the cricket ground alongside the Mardyke and the team of 'agile young men in flannels and blazers' on their way to play; the sound of piano practice emanating from a parlour window and the rhythms of a German band filling a bystreet; the gentility and ease associated with the efforts of a maid among the flowers on a sill. By way of contrast, Stephen has no real friends, plays no sports, neither sings nor plays (though Joyce did), and lives in increasingly unstable and squalid conditions.

Cork's bustle reflects cheer and industry, while Dublin's is associated in Stephen's mind with confusion and disorder. In addition, Cork is characterized for the most part by full daylight and sun, while every scene taking place in Dublin, with the exception of the journey to the Bull (which is illuminated by 'veiled sunlight'), takes place either in dull light or at night. The only other sunny day mentioned in the novel is the backdrop for Stephen's bout of illness at Clongowes, and Joyce uses this as the opportunity for an ironic discovery: 'You could die just the same,' Stephen muses, 'on a sunny day.' The essence of this observation applies equally well to the visit in Cork.

There was another source of irony available to Joyce, though Stephen does not mention it, in the fact that the grounds of Queen's College adjoin the county gaol. John Joyce had entered Queen's in 1867 with the intention of becoming a doctor. Instead, he became an actor, fiddler, singer, sportsman and *bon vivant:* a virtuosity incorporating the elements of its own dissipation. It must have occurred to Joyce that the contiguity of the college and the gaol was symbolically appropriate, especially since his father liked to paint himself a prisoner of circumstance, hostage to his wife and children.

One other point which deserves attention is the train route. As father and son leave Kingsbridge (Heuston) station in Dublin, Stephen recalls his first day at Clongowes. Though Joyce does not say so, the train to Cork passes through Sallins about an hour outside of Dublin and is, therefore, the same route Stephen took earlier on his way to the college. The way Joyce has Stephen relate the two events in his mind is an example of the manner in which the author uses place to convert the simple narrative into a complex of related feelings, in this case, again, to draw the line between present and past, innocence and experience.

Opposite Top: Entrance at Queen's College, Cork (Lawrence Collection, NLI).

Bottom: The Mardyke Walk, Cork, traversed by Stephen and his father to and from Queen's College.

The Labyrinth (pp. 96-101; 136-146)

Joyce was considered a serious and promising student at Belvedere, especially, as time went on, in English literature, and he took prizes for every year except 1896 when he neither attended school regularly nor sat for the examinations. It is the cheque awarded in 1897 which Stephen cashes in the episode following the trip to Cork. In one of the fine ironies connected with his schooling, Joyce places Stephen's family in Foster Place. This short street was named in honour of the last speaker of the Irish Commons, John Foster, later Lord Oriel who, though not the most reactionary man of his day, nevertheless opposed the abolition of the penal laws which placed serious restrictions on the education of Catholic boys like Stephen, and made it impossible for them to distinguish themselves by taking academic honours in their own country. Interestingly, it was the disestablishment of the Anglican Church in Ireland and the dispersal of their excess liquid assets which originally provided the funds for the examination awards.

Stephen and his father enter the bank and after cashing his 'orders on the governor of the Bank of Ireland' for £33, Simon Dedalus lingers to point out to his son that the great hall in which they stand was the House of Commons of the Irish parliament until its dissolution in 1800 with the Act of Union. Much altered since that time, it still inspires Dedalus to compare unfavourably the politicians of the present day with those of an earlier age. Henry Flood and John Hely Hutchinson had both been celebrated men, known at one time as the chief author and the butt, respectively, of two famous satirical volumes. Flood's *Baratriana* (1772) was aimed at the administration of the viceroy of the hour, and *Pranceriana* criticized Hutchinson, appointed provost of Trinity college in

1774, for tampering with the curriculum thenceforth to include dancing classes among other frills, for which he was nicknamed 'The Prancer'. Both of these volumes contained the kind of satire and word-play Joyce was fond of. Grattan and Flood also led efforts to make Ireland more independent of English legislative domination in the late eighteenth century. In 1887 this particular political pot was on the simmer, and to John Joyce, the lost Parnell embodied the sum total of great men in his own experience.

Opposite the bank on Foster Place stood the building known 100 years before as Daly's Club. In its time it was the grandest gambling house in Europe, garnering a substantial number of clients

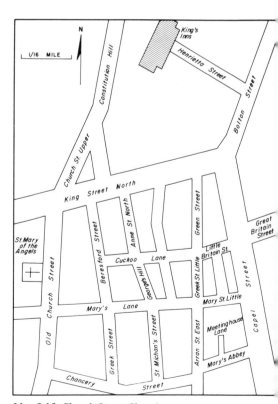

Map 2.10. Church Street Chapel.

'Stephen's mother and his brother and one of his cousins waited at the corner of quiet Foster Place.'

search for some object for his sexual tension. This area included Montgomery, Tyrone and Mabbot Streets, now renamed and transformed in character, and a warren of narrower laneways, most of which are gone entirely. Only Mabbot Lane and Beaver Street retain their original names and recall the once lively district which contained innumerable houses of prostitution, some elegant and well-maintained and some extremely degraded. This area had been handsome and aristocratic in the eighteenth century but the construction of the Custom House at its present easterly site hastened the removal of its more well-to-do residents and brought about its eventual decline. By 1860 it was notorious,

from the parliament next door. Stephen's proximity to this establishment underscores his improvidence, which begins immediately. Dismissing the notion of buying a new coat for his shivering mother (Barnardo's was — and is — nearly as close to Foster Place as 'Underdone's'), he leads the family across to Church Lane where they are to dine at the Burlington Hotel and Oyster Rooms, latterly a bank premises but undergoing renovation (opposite St Andrews). The mention of Barnardo's also recalls the famous nineteenth-century philanthropist Dr Thomas John Barnardo (1845-1905), who established 'Barnardo Homes for homeless children', and underscores Stephen's lack of real charity.

As Stephen's money and his best-laid plans depart, he is driven again to walk the streets and alleys of Monto (so-called after one of its principal streets, Montgomery) in

'God help us! he said piously . . . Hely Hutchinson and Flood and Henry Grattan . . . and the noblemen we have now, leaders of the Irish people at home and abroad.' Henry Grattan statute before the old parliament.

not only in Dublin but throughout Europe, for its brothels and drinking houses, its madams, prostitutes, fancy men and bullies, and thieves. It was entirely unregulated by corporation or constabulary and sniffed at by the more upright citizens of Dublin, at least in public, but it was visited by all classes of men from wealthy merchants and gentry to students and shop assistants. The city, after a few half-hearted attempts at rehabilitation (among them changing the names of the streets, which inconveniences the student of this period more than it did the habitués), finally wiped out business with virtually one fell swoop, though with the passage of time and several of its more able madams, and with the efforts of various benevolent groups and reformers, the old pace had gradually slackened of its own accord.

The decline of Monto took place after the period about which Joyce writes, though Stephen, in the grip of adolescent fears and fires, concentrates on its seamier sights, characterizing the district by its 'dark slimy streets' and the 'gloom of lanes and doorways' from which emanated the riot of drunks and brawlers and the calls of women and girls who 'dressed in long vivid gowns traversed the street from house to house'. The latter were employed in the lower-class, open-door establishments, and as drink could be bought at all hours of the day or night, disorderliness was common among the former.

The picture Joyce paints of Monto and of Stephen's tortured behaviour bears a resemblance to the dream of his own private hell which drives him, after the third day of the school retreat, to search out a place where he can confess. Stephen makes this single foray west of Sackville (O'Connell) Street, but Joyce frequently walked at least as far as Capel Street to one of the two corporation libraries: the one at the north end of Capel Street near Great Britain (Parnell) Street — so he was familiar with the area.

Very likely Stephen follows Great Britain Street west, movement antithetical to the seaward walk at the end of Chapter Four not only in direction (and remember that Joyce associates westward movement with entrapment) but also by implication, that is, Great Britain Street, along with Summerhill and Ballybough Road, comprised the ancient road north to the sea.

Church Street is a very old thoroughfare, heart of the oldest part of the city north of the Liffey, and its environs meshed perfectly with Stephen's preoccupation with the figure of the Virgin and with his figurative descent beyond the lowest strata of human existence. This street was at the western limit of the estate of the great St Mary's Abbey, whose abbot and monks held spiritual and temporal sway from the Liffey to Drumcondra during the Middle Ages. No vestige of the abbey remains on Mary's Abbey Street — it was pulled down to provide building material for the first Essex Bridge — but the chapter house was accessible from Meetinghouse Lane, and the influence of St Mary's is reflected in the names of several nearby streets: Mary's Lane, Mary Street and Abbey Street. Afterwards the district housed a market which was often the rallying point for the Catholic guilds in their sporadic clashes with the Protestants of the liberties south of the river. It also enjoyed an era of fashionability centred about Capel Street and, more expressive of Stephen's dilemma, is associated with the administration of justice: the Four Courts looming next to the Liffey between Church Street and Chancery Place, and the King's Inns skirting the area to the north.

By the end of the nineteenth century these streets were dominated by commerce: the potato market on Great Britain Street, the Mason's and Norfolk Markets between Moore Street and Coles Lane, the Rotunda Market on Coles Lane, and further west, the fruit market off Anglesea Row and

'Stephen looked at his thinly clad mother and remembered that . . . he had seen a mantle . . . in the window at Barnardo's' — number 108, far left. (Lawrence Collection, NLI).

Little Green Street, the fish market and the great Corporation market established in 1892 on opposite sides of St Michan's Street. In addition, there were countless stalls, barrows and bins of every description; whole streets given over to the purveyors of small articles, their businesses climbing the walls and spilling over in the path of milling shoppers and idling barefoot children. Today, carters and warehouse-men block the pavement in St Michan's Street, and Moore Street dimly recalls the redolence of fish and spirits and wet sawdust that Stephen remarks on, but Henry Street alone throngs with shoppers. The rest eke out an indeterminate course, shabby but infinitely more sedate than in the closing years of the last century.

Side by side with the markets and the numerous foundries, mills, and distilleries which were also found in this area, were a widow's asylum, a widow's almshouse and an orphan's institution, all between Chapel Lane and Little Denmark Street, and in Stephen's path as he crossed to Church Street. The presence of these institutions and the conditions under which the inmates and their fellow creatures in the streets and behind the stalls lived combine in the figure of the old woman who points the way to the Church Street chapel. Her demeanour gives us some sense of why, apart from his desire for anonymity, Joyce does not have Stephen confess at the school chapel or at St Francis Xavier's Church (where his family were communicants), which was a relatively fashionable parish. It was in this area that he brushed shoulders with people more humble, more abased than he, who could be, as he was forced to admit, more beloved of God than he. This is the nadir of his pride.

The Capuchin Church of St Mary of the Angels (called the Church Street chapel) lies on the west side of Church Street above May Lane. Stephen arrives during the evening hours, but even in the daytime the church is only dimly lit — its windows are high up on the left in the main church and high on the right in the adjoining chapel. We must consider that Joyce had a daunting environment in mind for the penitent Stephen because he is in one real sense surrounded as soon as he steps into the nave. The confessional boxes dominate the left wall nearest the entrance and the opposite wall in the chapel. Also on his right are several niches, decorated and fitted with *prix dieux* and given over to the devotion of individual saints. The altar rises dim in the distance, more remote this evening because, as Joyce says, the candles had been extinguished. One other decorative feature probably influenced the narrative — certainly it is in keeping with the appearance of the workmen and it embraces Stephen's reflections on 'poor and simple people following a lowly trade, handling and shaping the wood of trees. . .', and on Christ as a carpenter 'cutting boards and planing them': that is the predominance of unpainted wood throughout the church, on the ceilings, in the furnishings and on the floors.

Chapter Three

WELCOME, O LIFE!

The Rising Ground Above the River
(pp. 147-164)

After a period of prodigious reformation Stephen comes to equate Catholicism and the humility he sought and found so palpably present in Church Street in a different way: exemplifying a dearth of spirit, an unregenerate grace. Thus, the suggestion that he embrace a religious vocation can only be viewed as an invitation to death. This Joyce makes abundantly clear both in the description of the interview and in the contrasting images which engage Stephen later.

The interview takes place in the parlour, which was on the first floor of Belvedere House. Because of the house's commanding position at the top of North Great George's Street hill, Stephen is well able to watch the summer light fading over the surrounding roofs. It is a sepulchral setting, befitting the spiritual torpor exhibited by the director, but it is also the venue of a triumph of self equal to that which Stephen achieved at Clongowes, as that institution and the victory hard won there are insinuated into the present situation by the author. The portraits in the parlour recall those in the 'dark narrow corridor'; the swish of the director's soutane announcing his presence is a warning reminiscent of that which preceded the pain and humiliation of the pandying. In both cases Stephen rejects the judgements of his superiors.

As Stephen comes out onto the steps in front of the college a group of young men, striding and swaying in time to the music of a concertina, comes from the direction of Findlater's Church, just west of Belvedere on the corner of Rutland (Parnell) Square and North Frederick Street. Their casual high spirits are a marked and prophetic contrast to the gravity and joylessness of the director and to the spare grey façade of the Jesuit House on Upper Gardiner Street. Walking towards Drumcondra Bridge, Stephen traverses Dorset Street Lower, Binn's Bridge and Drumcondra Road Lower, passing St Alphonsus's Convent on the latter. St Alphonsus, it will be remembered, was the author of the book Stephen used for his 'visits to the Blessed Sacrament'. Joyce's description of the volume — 'a neglected book. . . . with fading characters and sere foxpapered leaves' — finds its echo in the statue of the Blessed Virgin, bereft of glory, standing 'fowlwise on a pole' among the poor cottages on the south bank of the Tolka. Stephen has ceased to romanticize the figure of the Virgin, and the book, evocative of 'a faded world of fervent love and virginal responses', has lost its power to stay his re-emergence into the world of natural temptations. The 'hamshaped encampment' is gone now, replaced by a neat park and a newer, more sterile version of Mary, but a memorial of the kind Joyce mentions can be seen nearby, beyond number 210 Clonliffe Road.

Joyce is careful here to delineate Stephen's physical surroundings, emphasizing that the disorder he encounters has begun to have greater appeal for him than the artificial order he sought earlier and that which distinguished a religious vocation. By omitting to mention that Stephen

41

is in fact entering a district familiarly known as the 'Holy Land' because of the number of religious institutions in the area, Joyce enhances the overriding importance of its natural features. It is natural rather than spiritual forces which motivate the characters in this setting, and while there exists no evidence of real vigour or animation, the process glimpsed by the boy is looked upon as a hopeful one.

The fields above the river were even then being built over, but they still retained a country atmosphere, including the mucky lanes and spilled over kitchen gardens, particularly in the vicinity of Millbourne Villas, which was across the road from and a little beyond the orderly pattern of houses reaching west from the crossroads between Drumcondra Road Upper and Lower. The Joyces' neighbours were small farmers and working-class and were not comfortable with the Joyces, who had too much of the air of the superior, but temporarily embarrassed, middle class. Stanislaus Joyce portrays the neighbourhood in pastoral terms, remembering the woods, fields and streams where the children played. A piece of the Tolka then flowed much nearer number two, which sat at the foot of the rising ground above the river between the grounds of St Patrick's Training College and the present location of Ferguson Road. In light of the fact that Stephen is now leaving behind the allegiances of his boyhood, it is a small thing, but interesting, to note that St Patrick's College occupied a building known formerly as Belvidere House.

Joyce has Stephen turn left into the lane which led to his home as soon as he has crossed the bridge. Though it was possible to follow the riverside and turn up a lane which ran from below Millmount Avenue straight through to Millbourne, he probably refers to a little treed alleyway which ran behind a wall on the north side of Millbourne to his doorstep and beyond. Tracing this route is further complicated

by the fact that Millbourne Avenue was at the time called Millbourne Lane throughout its length.

Stephen enters the house to learn that his mother and father are again looking for new quarters. This address and all subsequent addresses are outside the circuits of the Tolka and Liffey and the two Dublin canals. A look at the map shows how they girdle the city and in Stephen's reference they might be termed twin tourniquets on the all but bloodless city centre. Getting outside the ring is an important symbolic step for Stephen and it very appropriately coincides with his escape from the 'guardians of his boyhood', his parents and the church, who 'had sought to keep him among them that he might be subject to them and serve their ends'. Ireland, and its microcosm Dublin, might be expected to extract a similar toll. Davin makes that clear in Chapter Five.

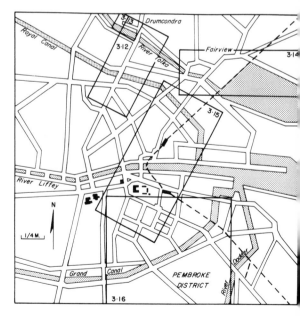

Map 3.11 Locating Maps 3.12 (Drumcondra); 3.13 (Millbourne Lane); 3.14 (Fairview and Bull Wall); 3.15 (Walk across the city); 3.16 (South of the Liffey).

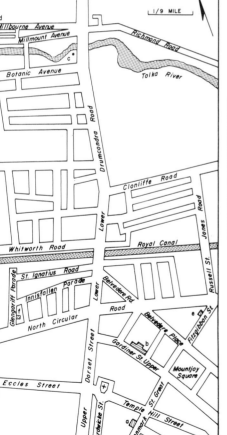

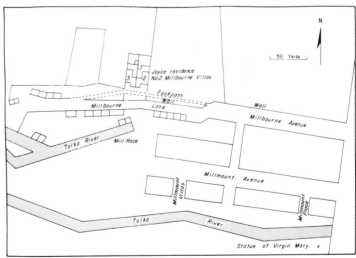

Belvedere College door — 'the heavy hall door'. (left).

Towards Findlater's church (centre).

The 'faded blue shrine of the Blessed Virgin which stood focalwise on a pole in the middle of a hamshaped encampment of poor cottages.'' (right).

Map 3.12. Drumcondra: (a) Belvedere College; (b) St Francis Xavier Church and Jesuit Residence; (c) Statue of the Blessed Virgin; (d) No. 2 Millbourne Lane, Joyce residence (1894); (e) 14 Fitzgibbon Street, Joyce residence (1893); (f) 32 Glengariff Parade, Joyce residence (1901)
Map 3.13. Millbourne Lane.

The Ancient Kingdom of the Danes
(pp. 164-173)

Significantly, the family now moves to a house close to the sea, the first move in that direction since they have been in the city. The new house, called 'Stella Maris', was north of Fairview Strand at 29 Windsor Avenue. Probably the most important, and most obvious, topographical element in the final episode of Chapter Four is the fact that Stephen reaches the sea. Every other aspect of the setting, however, contributes to the achievement of the 'luminous silent stasis' represented by Stephen's encounter with the girl on the strand.

29 Windsor Avenue.

The conflict at the beginning of this section is between Stephen's own unfolding purpose and all other authority — home, church and country. Joyce begins by placing Stephen between Patrick Byron's public house on the south side of Ballybough bridge (and in the vicinity of one of the city's ancient outlets to the sea, the end of Ballybough Road) and the Clontarf Chapel (the Church of the Visitation) on the corner of Fairview Strand and Philipsburg Avenue, simultaneously delineating the nature of the argument going on between Stephen and his mother and establishing in symbolic terms two of the three objects of his rebellion. Typically, these symbols overlap. A single location, the publichouse, points not only to his long-standing fidelity to Byron but to his growing interest in literature, to the exclusion of most other school subjects. It also serves to represent his father, as the Church typifies the position of his mother.

Unable to wait any longer for the news concerning his admission to university he breaks across the bridge and around the corner past the police barracks at number two Fairview Strand (now relocated), thus leaving behind a third group of authority figures. What follows manifests how the narrative in *A Portrait* is both conditioned by and enhanced by Joyce's systematic use of the natural, historical, and even etymological attributes of a particular setting. Besides following the curve of Dublin Bay to the sea, the route from Fairview to the Bull provides a comprehensive view of the scenes of Stephen's boyhood. Here, at what he considers the turning-point in his life, he can see the quays and the city behind him, and south, all the way to the mountains. His surroundings were very flat, and relatively primitive, particularly as neared the Bull. Towards Howth, the shore cottages even now have the look of a fishing village and recall Mercedes once more, and Stephen's adolescent desire:

> He wanted to meet in the real world the unsubstantial image which his soul so constantly beheld. He did not know where to seek it or how, but a premonition which led him on told him that this image would, without any overt act of his, encounter him. They would meet quietly as if they had known each other and had made their tryst, perhaps at one of the gates or in some more secret place. They would be alone, surrounded by darkness and silence: and in that moment of supreme tenderness he would be transfigured. He would fade into

Left: *Clontarf chapel. Stephen passes 'beyond the challenge of the sentries who had stood as guardians of his boyhood' escaping past the chapel on his way way to Bull Island.* Right: *The bridge at Bull Island where he felt 'the planks shaking'.* Below: *The strand at Bull Island from the bridge — 'he tried to hide his face from their eyes by gazing down sideways into the shallow swirling water under the bridge.'*

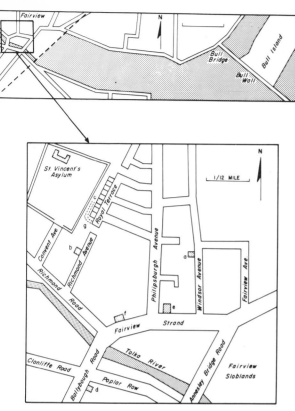

Map 3.14. Fairview and the Bull Wall: (a) 29 Windsor Ave., Joyce residence (1898); (b) 13 Richmond Ave., Joyce Joyce residence (1899); (c) 8 Royal Terrace, Joyce residence (1900); (d) Byron's publichouse; (e) Clontarf church; (f) police barracks; (g) lane behind the terrace.

something impalpable under her eyes and then in a moment, he would be transfigured. Weakness and timidity and inexperience would fall from him in that magic moment (p. 65).

This passage precedes the first great shift in direction Stephen experienced: that is his move into the city. It also presages the event about to take place in this expansive prelude to a new life.

To the Stephen contemplating a drastic break with the past and a step into an open and unknown future, the scene is daunting in some respects. Besides Joyce's allusions to the fragility of the plank bridge, to Stephen's dread of the 'cold, infrahuman

odour of the sea', to the precariousness of his assault on the 'spine of rocks' with which the Bull Wall terminated, the Dublin reader would have known that the shore falls off to the south in an indeterminate way and that the familiar city landmarks are largely obscured behind a jumble of wharfs and a smoke pall. The island itself, jutting well out into the bay, is sandy and wild and scarcely above the level of the sea anywhere, and though it represents a certain security to Stephen it provides virtually no protection or shelter. It was, however, the frequent haunt of sea birds, and this is conducive to Joyce's use of bird imagery.

Geographically, the situation bears a distant similarity to Joyce's conception of Stephen's development. The North Bull lies in Dublin Bay adjacent to the shore at Clontarf. This island and its sister, which was all but gone even in Joyce's time, were thrown up by the tensions between the rivers Liffey and Tolka, in whose orbit Stephen had spent the whole of his life, and the sea into which they open. Placing Stephen in the vicinity of the Bull also has a strong bearing on the flow of this section and on the quality of the prose. The sound of the sea at Clontarf can be so intense that early Scandinavian settlers named the islands after its roar. Its echo is particularly noticeable in the 'rhythmic rise and fall of words' and in the quality of the images:

He heard a confused music within him as of memories and names which he was almost conscious of but could not capture even for an instant; then the music seemed to recede, to recede, to recede: and from each receding trail of nebulous music there fell always one long-drawn calling note, piercing like a star the dusk of silence. Again! Again! Again! A voice from beyond the world was calling (p. 167).

With allusions to the 'thingmote' and to 'the ancient kingdom of the Danes' Joyce also allows historical associations to guide the reader. In particular this recalls the circumstances surrounding the defeat of the Scandinavians at the hands of Brian Boru on Good Friday, 28 April, 1014, after a lengthy period of occupation in and around Dublin. The final battle raged around the mouth of the Tolka and eastwards towards Clontarf. Boru, though victorious, did not survive the engagement. He was killed by a Danish admiral, an apostate from Christianity. This set of events significantly elaborates the narrative, introducing a Christ-figure, victor and victim, and an anti-Christ, victor and victim, which overlap each other and suffuse subsequent events — and incidentally interjects the influence of a pagan world in this 'seventh city of Christendom'.

As the gates and guardians of Stephen's boyhood recede into the distance, a new Stephen begins to rise in apposition to the gibes of the boys cavorting uninhibitedly in the bathing place between the east side of the Bull and the rude rock wall. Their incantation unites Stephen's passage from boyhood to young manhood, from spiritual bondage to spiritual freedom, from the prospect of a barren priesthood to the possibility of creative ascendancy with a triumverate of creeds focused around the ritual enactment of divine sacrifice. It is not the sacrificial but the redemptive elements of these creeds (Greek, Roman, Christian) which Joyce wishes to stress, however. The phrase *Bous Stephanoumenos* coupled with the symbol of the 'old artificer' suggests that Stephen enters this new phase of his existence glorified by the regalia of a new priesthood. Other elements suggest rebaptism and resurrection.

Seminal in the development of these textural devices is the Bull Island. Its pattern of associations gives impetus and validity both to Stephen's inclination towards a secular approach to life and to his gradual decision to escape. The power of myth succeeds the power of dogma in Stephen's panoply.

Morning Walk Across the City (pp. 174-204)

Much has been said about the Christ imagery in the final chapter of *A Portrait*, and it is assiduously present, but apart from the Royal (Inverness) Terrace address (where Stephen hears the mad nun's cries) and one or two other locations (Lower Mount Street, for example), the topography does not evoke or support this particular theme. Rather it is fundamentally related to the alienation/betrayal/departure superstructure of which the crucifiction theme is an element, and is central to the direction of the narrative. Further, topographical details illustrate the 'phases of apprehension' outlined during Stephen's walk with Lynch.

Joyce's use of place as impetus to the narrative is particularly evident in the first section (the walk across the city) and is conducive to the exercise of the stream-of-consciousness technique employed here. Both in the projected trip, which takes him from his house to Trinity College, and in the actual walk, from Newcomen Bridge to the University (they overlap), visual cues set off the train of thought which reflects and intensifies Stephen's growing desire to leave Ireland. In the first portion of the walk, the sloblands around the mouth of the Tolka (at Annesley Bridge), the shops on North Strand Road, the stone works on Talbot Place, the ship's provisioner's on Burgh Quay, and the Royal Theatre on Hawkins and Poolbeg Streets, which, incidentally, was across the street from a plaster and lath, mock-Tudor structure, not uncommon in Dublin, and nearby another Tudor establishment which came

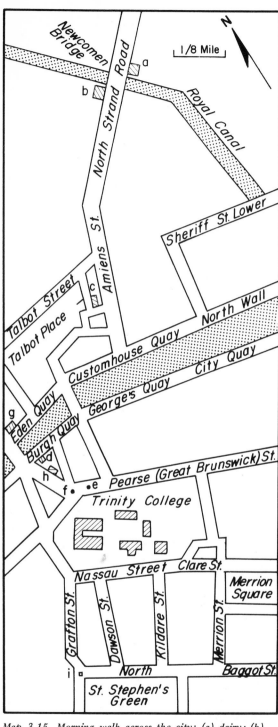

Map 3.15. *Morning walk across the city: (a) dairy; (b) newsagent's; (c) Baird's stone cutting works; (d) marine dealers shop; (e) Thomas Moore statue; (f) Sir Phillip Crampton memorial; (g) Hopkins & Hopkins, jewellers; (h) Dunn's of D'Olier Street; (i) Wolfe Tone slab.*

into being under a charter granted by Elizabeth I, Trinity College, remind Stephen of literary affinities: figures who in one way or another have something in common with him either in the style or quality of their works or in personal terms. All five – Hauptmann, Newman, Cavalcanti, Ibsen, Jonson – were inconoclasts. Two, Cavalcanti and Ibsen, were exiles because of their views; Jonson flirted with treason; Newman's years at the Catholic University followed upon the suggestion of heresy in his writings; Hauptmann travelled widely out of his native Silesia and was early condemned for his social criticism (as was Ibsen). Joyce noted in an early workbook (1903) that Stephen 'looked in vain for some poet of his generation to be his whetstone'. For Joyce, Hauptmann may have partially filled that need. They shared certain technical and ideological affinities (two of Hauptmann's plays published in 1899 and 1903, for example, took shape around heroes who were victims of their environments), and both owed something to the influence of Ibsen. The Norwegian playwright, whom Joyce studied seriously, even to the extent of trying to learn Dano-Norwegian (he also attempted the Silesian dialect of Hauptmann), and whom he reviewed while still in university and defended in Dublin literary circles, underwent a boyhood strikingly similar to Joyce's. Other parallels between Stephen/Joyce and these authors also existed: Cavalcanti was a sceptic in an age of religious fervour; Jonson protested his scruples against the taking of communion; all were alienated to a greater or lesser extent from their communities. We stress these personal parallels rather than certain artistic considerations because of the locations which call these figures to mind. In every case, Stephen is within easy access to some point of departure from Ireland, reinforcing the theme of alienation/exile already broached with the introduction of the five authors.

The sloblands at Fairview are transformed at high tide into Dublin Bay; North Strand Road gives onto the North Wall Quay from which a cross-sea ferry embarked; Talbot Place is across from Amiens Street (Connolly) Station, the railway link to Kingstown (Dun Laoghaire), the departure point for ferries to Holyhead; and the provisioner's at 2 Burgh Quay and theatre are virtually on top of the port of Dublin steam-packet companies, as well as being contiguous to the bay.

Other elements point to Stephen's imminent departure. The motivation for this move, implicit throughout the novel, is summarized in the final chapter. Between Newcomen Bridge and the university Joyce reviews the Irishry: 'The soul of the gallant venial city which his elders had told him of,' Stephen says, 'had shrunk with time to a faint mortal odour rising from the earth.' The scholar, the priest, the peasant, the poet, the patriot, the woman, all occupy a position in the Irish moral system which he feels is untenable and dishonest, and it is not difficult to infer this from the text. Joyce's own insurgency placed him outside all streams of accepted dogma, complicated as they were by religious parochialism and aggressive nationalism, and he deplored their excesses and distortions. The landmarks featured in the course of his walk to the university all enhance his convictions: the Ivy Church on North Strand Road associated with Fr Conmee in *Ulysses* dissolves into 'wayward rhythms' and a reminder that his 'monkish learning' is inadequate to his task; Trinity College, the Protestant bastion which, along with the Castle on the other end of Dame Street, stood perpetual watch over the privileges of the Protestant ascendancy '[sits] heavily in the city's ignorance'; the statue of Thomas Moore 'the national poet of Ireland' whose *Irish Melodies* made him an enormous success in his homeland, but who spent the majority of his life and talents among the English, is a 'Firbolg in

the borrowed cloak of a Milesian', a reference to successive groups of invaders of Ireland which corresponds to a central thematic statement, that is, he was not what he seemed to be; the mention of Grantham Street in relation to Davin the peasant/nationalist, associating his blind loyalty to 'the broken light of Irish myth' with the steadfastness of that other homeless group in his immediate purview, the Jews (the Jewish connection also affirms that like Simon Dedalus, his wife, and Stephen himself, all of whom lived at least part of their lives adjacent to Jews, Davin is complicit in his own victimization); Grafton Street, bustling with shoppers and tourists, prolonging 'that moment of discouraged poverty', and reminding him as he reaches its apex of the vain heroism of Wolfe Tone and the 'tawdry tribute' offered on a summer day in 1898 when a foundation stone was

The back of the house at 8 Royal Terrace. Stephen leaves the house on his 'morning walk across the city.'

set in festive memorial to the United Irishmen.

St Stephen's Green is especially evocative of that 'corruption' which Stephen senses pervading Dublin. In this case he refers to a smell of death. The corruption practised by Buck Egan and Burn-chapel Whaley was said to be Satan-worship, and it was rumoured that they conducted Black Masses in Whaley's mansion. This notion or the fact that 'Buck' Whaley, Burn-chapel's son, was involved with the Castle informant — and gutter journalist — Jack Higgins, gives rise to Stephen's feeling that the university hall is 'not unwatchful'. The theme of treachery which is a touchstone in his existence (and which informs his relations with Cranly and much else in this chapter) is bolstered by the fact that several scoundrelly characters are associated with the area. Captain O'Shea, for example, who betrayed the relationship between Parnell and Kitty O'Shea, attended the university at 86 St Stephen's Green. This same address was originally the home of the aforementioned Burn-chapel Whaley, the magistrate and notorious priest-hunter (who ironically swore that no Papist would ever cross his threshold) and Buck Whaley, boon-companion to Francis Higgins, whose nefarious contribution to the suppression of the Rising of 1798 perhaps exceeded in ignominy the Earl of Clonmell's defrauding of countless Catholics in land transactions, and Whaley's acceptance of £4000 bribe (he was one of the many who succumbed to the temptation) to vote with the Unionists in 1800. Higgins lived at 82 St Stephen's Green and Clonmell just around the south-west corner on Harcourt Street, though his holdings also included the garden behind Stephen's Green South — contiguous to the university garden (Cranly's handball game against the wall of the alley beside number 86 recalls a fabled wager which took Buck Whaley to Jerusalem to play ball against the city's walls).

The principal university building was characteristic of the 'grandiloquent' school

of architecture and assumed such proportions partly through the elder Whaley's desire to overshadow his neighbours. This pretentiousness is in keeping with other shams which Stephen notes from time to time. The university itself was a fraud in one respect, though as represented by the guttered Dean of Studies it was more pitiable than blameworthy. The curriculum offered therein was not demanding, its examinations requiring little more than those at Belvedere. Stephen responds with mild sarcasm and laxity with regard to attendance and his fellow-students with wrong-headedness and horseplay. As a matter of fact, the intellectual life of the university and the city in general was keener than Joyce admits, but these activities were largely extra-curricular and any mention of them would have been inimical to Joyce's purpose — which was, of course, to establish the widest possible breach between Stephen and his surroundings.

Opposite: *The Lane behind 8 Royal Terrace where he heard 'a mad nun's screeching in the nun's madhouse behind the wall'.* Above: *Entrance at 86 St Stephen's Green, 'the sombre college'.* Below: *The pond in St Stephen's Green (Lawrence Collections, NLI)*

Opposite: top: *The 'droll statue of the national poet of Ireland'. Thomas Moore was a 'Firbolg in the borrowed cloak of a Milesian';* left: *Entrance hall, 86 St Stephen's Green;* centre: *the stair hall from the landing. The door leads to the entrance hall; the corridor to the physics theatre is to the right of the picture;* Right: *the stair hall where the dean 'stood at the foot of the staircase, a foot on the l owest step . . .'* Above: *The garden behind the university. Stephen, Cranly and Temple cross the garden together, 'The president, wrapped in a heavy loose cloak, was coming towards them along one of the walks, reading his office.'*

South of the Liffey (pp. 204-247)

Opposite: *The canal bank above Leeson Bridge — 'a crude grey light, mirrored in the sluggish water, and a smell of wet branches over their heads seemed to war against the course of Stephen's thought.'* Above: *Where Stephen and Lynch join the many students 'sheltering under the arcade of the library'. At the right is Leinster House.*

The bulk of Chapter Five takes place between the university in St Stephen's Green and the national library on Kildare Street, boundaries consistent with Stephen's emerged intellectuality and relative maturity. His new freedom, or distance, from stress is reflected in the course of two walks, one with Lynch and the other with Cranly. The first takes Stephen and Lynch from the steps of the university to Leeson Street Bridge, delaying Stephen's escape outside the city limits but taking him east on a route which was predominantly taken westward via the canal barges which started at Ringsend and moved under Huband Bridge along the tree-lined canal to Portobello where they embarked passengers for the midlands and thus by the Shannon to Limerick. Appropriately enough, the discussion begins with Stephen's definition of beauty. The canal bank between Wilton Terrace and Warrington Place was a retreat in more than one sense, but here on the north side it lies considerably below the level of the street, providing the kind of tranquil background that properly reflects Stephen's own equilibrium (the noise of the dray rounding the corner near Sir Patrick Dun's Hospital and the meeting with Donovan distract Lynch and arouse his ire, but Stephen is unaffected).

Walking the length of Mount Street Lower, they turn at the north-west corner of Merrion Square and cross the street into Leinster Lawn, Stephen finishing his discourse on the creative process in the environs of the National Gallery (quite in keeping with Lynch's apparent philistinism, the gallery was, as George Moore remarked, like the Sahara: 'Now and then one sees a human being hurrying by like a Bedouin on the horizon.') and the School of Art (not the Royal Irish Academy, as Joyce says, which was on Dawson Street). In front of the library Stephen takes his place outside the group of students listening to their banter and exploring the feelings about

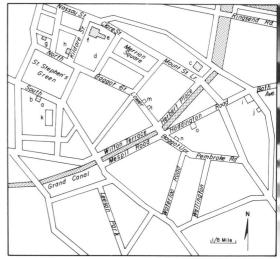

Map 3.16 South of the Liffey
(a)   *National University (also referred to as the Royal University and the Catholic University;*
(b)   *Alley behind the university;*
(c)   *St Patrick Dun's Hospital;*
(d)   *Duke's Lawn;*
(e)   *"Royal Irish Academy";*
(f)   *National Library;*
(g)   *Adelphi Hotel*
(h)   *Maple's Hotel*
(i)   *Infantry barracks ('Counterparts')*
(j)   *Farrington's house ('Counterparts')*
(k)   *Earlsfort Terrace Concert Room ('A Painful Case')*
(l)   *Private bank in Baggot Street ('A Painful Case')*
(m)   *Dan Burke's ('A Painful Case')*
(n)   *City of Dublin Hospital ('A Painful Case')*
(o)   *Haddington Road Church ('The Dead')*
(p)   *60 Shelbourne Road, Joyce residence (1904).*

his 'beloved' which are reflected in the succeeding passages, she becoming the focus, he the progenitor, of the verses beginning 'Are you not weary of ardent ways'.

The second long walk in this chapter begins with Stephen gazing across Kildare Street from the library steps at a covey of birds circling the cornice of a house in Molesworth Street. His preoccupation with symbols and portents is in part fostered by the appearance of the colonnade above him (also in part by the presence of those augur's impedimenta, the ashplant and the birds) and leads through thoughts associated with his assumption of the artist's role and his impending departure, culminating with his memory of the scene at the Antient Concert Rooms and the events surrounding the opening of Yeats's *The Countess Cathleen* (May 1899). Interrupted by the sound of gaslights coming on upstairs, he enters the round hall and ascends the stairs to the lofty reading room, finding Cranly at a table across from the desk. Stephen eventually goes ahead into Kildare Street and, while waiting for Cranly, notes the decadence of Ireland's 'patricians', a class he seems to have as little in common with (despite his father's admonitions) as he does with that represented by Cranly, who comes from a more unpretentious but equally decrepit background — a child of 'exhausted loins' from the 'decaying seaport', Wicklow. Kildare Street is an apt choice as a setting for these musings, as it was the location of a number of ascendancy establishments, the Maples Hotel at the top of the street (now gone) and the Kildare Street Club at the bottom among them, and was near several others. Also prominent was a mouldering statue of Queen Victoria in front of Leinster House. The walk with Cranly takes them from Kildare Street into Pembroke township (the area between the Grand Canal and Donnybrook) and back again to the vicinity of Leeson Park; in geographical terms, roughly the opposite of the one taken by Stephen and Lynch. It also takes the opposite emotional direction, tracing not what Stephen is embracing, but what he is fleeing from. Geographically, he leaves the city limits; emotionally, he is cutting all the rest of his ties. The break with Davin, one of his two intimates, comes before he sets off with Lynch; his link with Cranly, already tenuous at the outset of their conversation, slips away during its course. His other friends and acquaintances recede as well. Before he

goes off with Lynch he is a willing, though relatively subdued, participant in the raillery with his fellow students in the physics theatre, with MacCann and with Davin, until their disagreement becomes acrimonious. After the Lynch walk Stephen stands aloof from the others. The second walk, with Cranly, begins with Stephen purposefully disengaging himself from the others, going ahead of Cranly and then waiting for him, and ends some streets south of the university with intimations of his complete separation from his family and friends, from the city, the Church, Ireland itself — even from E--C--, whose influence, we see, is beginning to be inimical to his art. The emotional break with her is finalized in the Diary.

Two other topographical features are important to the narrative. First, as the route which Stephen and Cranly take traces one of the most ancient highways from Dublin to Blackrock, Kingstown (Dun Laoghaire) and Dalkey, Baggot Street and Pembroke Road obviously represent an escape route — one which Cranly attempts to cut off, both with his appeal to Stephen with regard to religious observance, to what is due to Stephen's mother, and to the dangers inherent in Stephen's position, and by physically altering their direction, turning Stephen back around northwards.

Secondly, Pembroke itself represents a complete antithesis to Stephen's own barren, beaten northern neighbourhoods, and a truce is established with Cranly as soon as they come under its influence. Its spaciousness and beauty, quiet and respectability, are reminiscent of Stephen's memories of Blackrock, before disorder overtook him. And they presage the new order which he sometimes sought though rarely achieved during his adolescence, but which he believes he will find in his new-found freedom and art.

Diary

Joyce once noted that the shortest way from the Cape of Good Hope to Cape Horn is to sail away from it. Rephrased, this serves as Stephen's testamentary farewell to Ireland: the shortest way to Tara, that eyrie of ancient Irish kings, was *via* Holyhead.

The Diary makes emphatic the careful distance of the author's stance. In the ultimate, 'dramatic' form of artistic expression, the artist, Stephen explained to Lynch, 'like the God of the creation, remains within or behind or beyond or above his handiwork, invisible, refined out of existence, indifferent, paring his fingernails'. Though Stephen's high lyricism, his increasing good humour, lend Dublin and everyone in it a benignity not heretofore present, he emerges in the first person to deliver a comprehensive *coup de grâce*.

Each setting, each episode, contains a rehearsal of one or more thematic elements, emphasizing the quality of life with which Stephen has so painfully forged an accommodation: the scene at the Rotunda on Rutland Square recalls the political cowardice and moral atrophy evident in the Parnell episode; his visit to the library uncovers yet another fallow argument reminiscent of those between various characters in Chapter Five; his stop at the cigar shop on North Frederick Street produces a last meeting with Davin, still the archpatriot (the famous meeting place of the Irish Irelanders was at 13 North Frederick Street and the headquarters of the Gaelic league on O'Connell, so it was appropriate that they should meet here), a last appearance of the elder Dedalus, still displaying his facile charm, still dispensing misplaced

advice, and with the mention of Findlater's Church, an echo of Stephen's first tenuous spiritual independence; the visit to the university produces another unarticulated dogmatic stand on the part of a churchman and another example of the worldly disposition of the Jesuits; the entry recording a scene at home re-emphasizes his mother's blind fealty to tradition and the extent of the breach between Stephen and this most fundamental attachment; the stop on Grafton Street, chronologically the last setting mentioned, reintroduces several themes, among them Stephen's ineluctable intimacy with women, and a co-identification between absurdly posturing patriots and deluded expatriots — the latter a reversal of the ' tame goose' represented by Davin, who talked vaguely of some future service to the French in imitation of the vaunted (Joyce would have said perverse) sixteenth century Wild Geese; Wicklow recalls the boy's early disillusion with the Ireland of his fathers and the despair of soul which characterizes Cranly, the child of that metaphorical pair of 'exhausted loins'; the West again represents Ireland's awesome grip on the sensitivities of even such a confirmed sceptic as Stephen.

Once again the city has played its role: setting, symbol, Stephen's correlative. It is not obtrusive, but it is definitely, concretely there, redefining the precise nature of Stephen's surroundings and his relationship to them. Like Joyce, who traversed Dublin again and again in his memory even after he had left it for good, Stephen ranges within its environs once more, this time with the wry moderation of one who has already escaped with his life.

PART TWO

DUBLINERS

Map 4.17. Dublin and environs.
The inset labelled c on this overview of Dublin City and its suburbs conscribes nearly all of the action in the fifteen stories of Dubliners. *The two exceptions are* "A Painful Case", *which takes in Chapelizod and the Phoenix Park to the west, and* "After the Race", *which begins along the Naas Road and concludes at the port of Dun Laoghaire, south-east of Blackrock.*

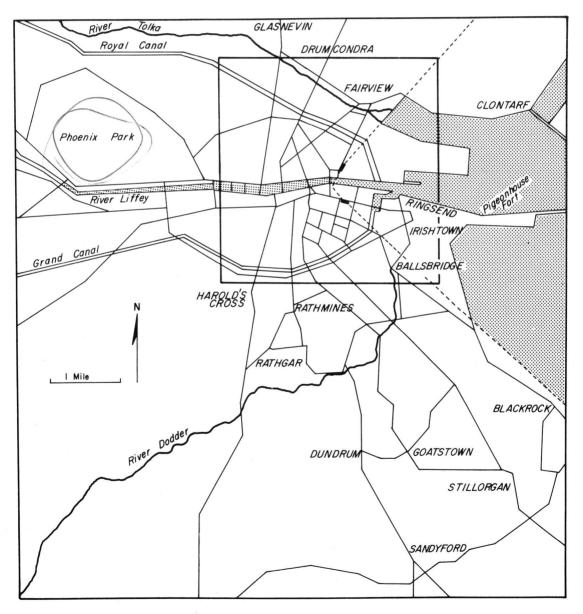

There is much to be gained from studying the topographical detail of *Dubliners*. In the first place, anyone with the necessary information to actually walk around Dublin tracing the characters' movements will increase his ability to visualize the stories as well as enrich his appreciation of Joyce's art. Granted, many of the landmarks Joyce mentions are gone from modern Dublin and the city, rebuilt extensively during this century, has in many places a markedly different quality from the city Joyce cast as the 'centre of paralysis'. Yet much of the Dublin he captured remains. The house on Usher's Island which serves as the location for 'The Dead' is there, a seed-merchant's office still occupying the ground floor. North Richmond Street, with the detached two-storey house still standing at its blind end, has likewise suffered little from renovation: the Christian Brothers' School, the laneways behind the houses, 'Joe Dillon's' back garden where the boys in 'An Encounter' play at 'Wild West' — these all seem to evoke the same resonances when standing on the street as can be felt when reading the stories set there. A walk from North Richmond Street into Ringsend and towards the Pigeon House, a pint in O'Neill's (now The Norseman) or Mulligan's, the view of the wall of Phoenix Park and the Liffey winding its way into Dublin while standing on the crest of Magazine Hill where James Duffey stood — all of this and more is available to those who wish to search it out. But having established the place and movement of Joyce's characters on the real map of turn-of-the-century Dublin, having assiduously followed the trail of these characters, having noted the boarding house in Hardwicke Street, the site of Mr Kernan's fall in the bar on Adam's Court, the location of the Dublin-by-Lamplight Laundry from which Maria sets out, and the building at number 15 Wicklow Street where Joyce has the 'committee' meet on Ivy Day, we have still only scratched the surface as regards the importance of topography to his first book.

It has already been suggested in broad outline that Joyce uses his characters' movements in *Dubliners* to create a unity among his stories (see Brewster Ghiselin, 'The Unity of Joyce's *Dubliners*'), but the closer analysis made possible when the stories are set on maps allows us to see an importance here which has not often been recognized. Since there is no doubt that Joyce was well aware of the mood topography could elicit, and since he knew too that his Dublin readers would be very familiar with the settings he calls up in each story, it is highly unlikely he would have failed to see the possibility of using these real details as one of the structural and symbolic elements of his book. In fact, there is an overall pattern which emerges in his use of place and movement which is essential to a full understanding of both his technique and his central point.

The first three stories ('stories of my childhood', Joyce called them) all emenate from North Richmond Street where the boy is an integral part of his environment; indeed, the environmental elements seem to conspire in an attempt to keep him attached to place: to home, to school, to country. The repeated and frustrated attempts at escape always place the boy in conflict with his surroundings: a journey east to the sea is opposed to the daily walk west to Belvedere College; the rules and restrictions of the Church are set against dreams of Persia and the sunny East; the three-cornered box of the dead-end street is contrasted with the quest for Eastern enchantment. In this way Joyce is able to suggest both an innate urge for escape and the manner in which the various factors comprising life in Dublin contrive to paralyze this urge.

In direction the movement of the first three stories always tends towards the east, but the matter is not as simple as it might at first appear. The movement away from the paralytic priest and all he represents in 'The Sisters' takes the boy directly east, but it takes him to a dead-end street and to a home where he is encouraged only to 'box his own corner'. Thus, we watch him oscillate east and west within a fairly restricted area and between two points which both operate to entrap him. He feels a 'sensation of freedom' when moving east, but is too young and too closely controlled by his environment to do much beyond noting the feeling. In the second and third stories the boy attempts to break out of his corner, at first with a companion and then on his own, and both movements are south-east and towards the sea. In each case, however, the movement culminates in an abrupt turn back to the west and ends in disappointment and frustration. We finally recognize that when the Dubliner as child is most prepared psychologically to escape the paralysis confronting him, he is least prepared to overcome the outside forces holding him in place. As we move further into the collection, other, more subtle, 'nets' are flung to entrap the characters.

The next two sections of *Dubliners*, as Joyce conceived the total work, consist of four stories examining the adolescent in Dublin, followed by four stories concentrating on adult life. In their use of topography and movement, these sections form parallel units which lead directly to the stasis dominating the three stories devoted to public life. In the first adolescent story 'Eveline', and in the first adult story, 'A Little Cloud', we are presented with characters who both have a strong urge to move to the east — Eveline because she believes a new life with Frank awaits her in Buenos Ayres, and Little Chandler because he thinks London or Paris will free him from his 'sober inartistic life'. Unlike the boy in the first three stories, both these characters are alienated from their immediate environments, their jobs, their fellow workers, and their families. As a result there is little in the way of a physical barrier keeping either from escape. Eveline lives in a north-eastern suburb of Dublin where changes in her family and neighbourhood have left her estranged and out of place. Little Chandler lives in the city centre but in a house where he is resented and which in turn he resents. Both believe that a ship from the North Wall represents their only chance for the lives they want, but neither can overcome the psychological nets which hold them paralyzed. We see Eveline 'helpless and passive' at the end and are left with the same picture of Little Chandler. In both stories, however, the movement is direct and purposeful up to a point; it corresponds to the eastward direction of each character's urge and comes up against a mental barrier which cannot be overcome.

'Eveline' is followed by two stories, 'After the Race' and 'Two Gallants', where the movement to the east becomes more indirect and the desire for escape less urgent, until it culminates in the aimless and circular wanderings of Lenehan and Corley. These stories are paralleled in the adult section by 'Counterparts', with its own circling of the city's pubs, and by 'Clay', where the drift west to east of 'After the Race' is counterbalanced by movement east to west, and where both central characters are pathetic victims of self-deception. The adolescent section ends with 'The Boarding House' where Bob Doran remains static; he wants to escape but cannot imagine how to effect it. The adult section closes with 'A Painful Case', with James Duffey equally static and alone in the north-western quadrant of the city watching the goods train out of Kingsbridge Station winding slowly to the west.

This sets the scene for the three stories of public life, 'Ivy Day in the Committee Room', 'A Mother', and 'Grace', where the characters have become all but stationary. They either remain in place, their imaginations grounded in the past, or they are so much a part of their lives in Dublin that we see them as static characters with neither the urge, the opportunity nor the energy to escape. The first and second of these stories play out all their action just south of the Liffey, and the third begins in a bar located in the city centre, and moves quickly to the north-west where the central character spends most of the story lying in bed. In the final story, 'The Dead', not originally intended as part of the collection, Joyce moves the scene across the Liffey to Usher's Island and has the characters remain in one place until the end, when they move west to the very centre of Dublin (the Gresham Hotel on O'Connell Street) and in their imaginations far to the West and into the past where the snow of paralyzing death covers all, living and dead, Dublin and Ireland, the whole universe.

The overall movement in *Dubliners* can be characterized as beginning with urgent attempts to escape the daily routine, attempts related to movement eastward and towards the sea, followed by an almost frantic desire to escape entrapment in Dublin by flight to the east, England and the Continent. This movement slackens, becomes indirect, circular and wandering, then changes to a westward tendency ending in stasis as death comes to dominate the characters' imaginations. It has been universally recognized that the opening

paragraph of 'The Sisters' serves as a microcosm of the whole collection, particularly where the boy is fascinated by paralysis and wishes 'to look upon its deadly work'. This also serves, however, as an indication of the movement in *Dubliners*, and it seems that Joyce wished to construct a composite picture of the quintessential Dubliner, showing him in all the stages of his 'paralysis' from the earliest stirrings to escape to the final image of Gabriel Conroy reconciled to begin his own 'journey westward'.

Little has been written about Joyce's adherence to the Dublin he knew in his collection of short stories, though a good deal has been said about his naturalistic technique in *Ulysses*. Magalaner and Kain (*Joyce: The Man, the Work, the Reputation*) suggest the same technique was at work in *Dubliners* and find it worth investigation:

While there is no special virtue in slavish adherence to truth of environmental background, in a creative work, at the same time Joyce's fidelity to the facts of Dublin as a physical entity should be recognized. Though the contest itself may not be the center of interest in 'After the Race', it is exciting to recognize that not only did such a race take place but that young Joyce was commissioned to cover a like event for the local newspaper [actually he interviewed a driver who was to take part in that race] . . . . Again Joyce sets one of his most memorable scenes in *Dubliners* in Corless' restaurant, where Little Chandler is made to feel more and more an outsider, a frustrated provincial, by his successful cosmopolitan friend, Gallaher. It has often been assumed that for this scene at least, the writer had created the setting from his imagination. Yet examination of *Thom's Official Directory of . . . Ireland* for 1896 shows this item: 'Corless,

Thomas, wine merchant and proprietor Burlington dining rooms, 24, 26, and 27 St. Andrew Street' and later reference to the place as 'Burlington Restaurant and Oyster Saloons'. Since Joyce writes the 'People went there after the theatre to eat oysters and drink liquers,' it is reasonable to suppose that once more he preferred to deal, like Zola, with a maximum of observable fact in his fiction (pp. 66-7).

Had these two critics searched further they might have been equally interested to find that in 1903 the Jammett Brothers purchased the Burlington Hotel and Oyster House from Corless and, replacing 'Oyster House' with the word 'Restaurant', altered its character so that *Thom's* lists it subsequently as a 'high-class French restaurant'. Thus, when Gallaher's talk turns to Paris and the Moulin Rouge and he calls the bartender 'Francois', Joyce clearly has these second owners in mind as well. In fact Joyce creates his own Corless's out of the characteristics of the two restaurants he knew at St Andrew's Street during his years in Dublin.

But surface naturalism is not the only level on which we can appreciate Joyce's use of topography. On learning, for example, that Corless's is on St Andrew's Street, is it coincidence only that this story takes place in late autumn (St Andrew's feast day is November 30), that Chandler's walk crossing the Liffey at Grattan Bridge inscribes a cross saltire (St Andrew's emblem), that this walk from King's Inn to Church Street suggests a religious allegory with elements of both the walk and Chandler's thoughts corresponding to elements in the lives of St Thomas Becket and St Thomas More, that the two central characters remind us in their names and roles in the story of St Ignatius of Loyola and St Thomas the Apostle, that the discussion in the bar centres on immorality in foreign capitals, and that Gallaher (a debased St Ignatius) claims to be privy to 'the secrets of religious houses on the Continent'? Or are these, in fact, all part of an intricate scaffolding of interrelationships and correspondences which many have seen as essential to Joyce's later prose technique?

These are the kinds of issues this study wishes to raise. It begins with several questions about Joyce's use of Dublin and his own and others' experiences there: How much of the environmental background does he create purely from his imagination and how much does he take from observable fact about the city? If he alters the reality of the Dublin he knew, does he do so for important structural reasons which should therefore command our special attention? If stories like 'Counterparts', 'Grace', 'A Mother' and 'An Encounter' are demonstrably based on actual incidents, does the creative process seem to depend on Joyce's setting these incidents where they really took place or does he feel free to move away from biographical reality in order to introduce topographical imagery or symbolism? Of particular interest, it may be possible to see the realistic details of the settings he chooses (though these details are often left unstated) suggesting structure, even incident, for some of his stories. 'Clay', for instance, may have begun in Joyce's mind as an examination of Maria of the Dublin-by-Lamplight Laundry on an evening's excursion to a relative's house. Since Maria was a relative of Joyce's mother on the Murray side of the family, it seems natural for him to have decided to make her travel, as she does in the story, to his Uncle John Murray's home at 55 St Brigid's Road in Lower Drumcondra. Having decided on this as the basic structure, might not the extensive use of saints' names for the streets where Maria finds herself called the element of All Saints' Day Eve to Joyce's mind, and a convent in turn have suggested the game of the three dishes which came to dominate the story? On the other hand the overall structure of stories like 'Ivy Day in the Committee Room' seems to suggest the individual elements of the setting. Joyce's siting of the 'committee' meeting on Wicklow Street, in a room at number 15 on the anniversary of Parnell's death, are all deviations from biographical reality which he added to support the story's central point.

It is surprising to see the number of stories where important topographical details are left unstated. Sometimes it is the quality of the surroundings, as in 'An Encounter' or 'Clay'; sometimes it is the name of a pub or the character of a restaurant, as in 'Two Gallants' or 'Grace' or 'A Little Cloud'; often it is the historical associations called up by a particular location or a particular building where the characters are placed, as in 'A Painful Case' or 'After the Race' or 'The Dead'; and sometimes it is what lies beyond the characters' movements, what they never achieve but what we should know lies in the direction they are heading.

It can of course be argued that if Joyce had wished us to have these details he would have supplied them, but it should be remembered he was writing this book for a Dublin audience. It was the Dubliner, he said, who needed a good look at himself, and the Dubliner reading these stories would have seen much that eludes the modern reader. He would have easily guessed the location and name of the bar where Mr Kernan falls and injures his tongue. He would recognized at once the importance of M'Auley's as a meeting place in that story and probably would have echoed Joyce's aunt who wrote to her nephew to say she knew how the story would end. The Dubliner would have placed Bob Doran immediately at the only boarding house on Hardwicke Street and would have known where the Catholic Wine Merchant's Office was located where Doran worked. The Dubliner would have been aware that the Vitriol Works at

Annesley Bridge was a manure processing plant and have been duly prepared for the degeneration of mood which follows the introduction of that image in 'An Encounter'. He would have been familiar with the quality of Ringsend, Irishtown and Chapelizod, Ballsbridge and Donnybrook, and would have called to mind the picture Joyce wished to create. He would have known which pubs really existed and which were fictitious (such as the Black Eagle), and therefore perhaps suggestive of some earlier gathering spot. He would have identified Ségouin's hotel and the location of the committee room and the neighbourhood where Eveline lived; he would have known of the English car placed last in the Gordon Bennett cup race and would have remembered the Grand Irish Concert at the Antient Concert Rooms where the accompanist left during the Saturday night performance and the second tenor, James Joyce, had to play the piano for himself.

So this study is also an attempt to bring back into focus the details of turn-of-the-century Dublin as Joyce would have expected his readers to know it. Some of the details relating to the short stories are now beyond reach, but much that will be of interest to those who study Joyce is available, and an attempt has been made to set it down with the accuracy Joyce would have demanded. The organization of this study, however, does not follow Joyce's arrangement of the stories in *Dubliners*. His plan was to show the 'paralysis of Dublin' at work on four separate groups characters, and in the first eleven stories he concentrates in turn on children, adolescents and adults. He follows these with three stories which deal with public life and concludes with 'The Dead', the longest and, in many ways, the most complex story in the book. Our concern is with geographical and topographical considerations.

The first section, 'North Richmond

Street Being Blind', deals with his first four stories, taking them together because the first three emanate from North Richmond Street where Joyce lived as a child and the fourth, 'Eveline', moves across essentially the same map to end at the North· Wall Station. Though Stanislaus Joyce insists in *My Brother's Keeper* that of these only 'An Encounter' has any relation to Joyce's personal experience, Joyce himself called the first three, 'stories of my childhood', and subsequent biographical study has suggested that Stanislaus was not always the best judge of what motivated his brother's work. 'The Sisters', for example, seems to be based, in part at least, on relatives Joyce knew when the family lived in Blackrock, and 'Araby', though it is drawn from incidents which occurred over a three-year period, uses neighbours Joyce knew as a child, accurate topographical detail, and a bazaar he actually attended. 'Eveline' is also based on real people who populate a real place, and his shift in that story from North Richmond Street to the neighbourhood of Fairview was essential to the overall structure of his book.

The second section, 'Fifty-Six Whiskeys', groups together four stories belonging geographically to the city centre and to the pubs and bars of the city. These stories develop incidents which happened to the adults who populated Joyce's years in Dublin: his father, his uncle William Murray, their neighbours and cronies. Joyce builds his characters, however, on composites of those he knew — choosing a trait here, a often-retold anecdote there, to create figures who are not, as he once worried they might be, simply caricatures of real people. Each character takes on a life of his own, and parallels with individuals Joyce knew are drawn in this study to comment on his technique rather than to assert he was writing autobiography.

The third section, 'Snow is General',

takes up the four stories in which the characters remain essentially in one place. The title, of course, comes from 'The Dead' where it represents, among other things, the static and immutable nature of the past, experience held in time where it works its inevitable effect on the present. The characters represented in these stories are caught up in the ganglia of their own parts or in the living force of their country's past, and struggle as they might, they cannot escape. By setting these stories where he does, Joyce increases his characters' entrapment, often calling up the topographical details of an older Dublin to aid him in his work.

The final section, 'Where the Corkscrew Was', deals with those stories which take place in suburban Dublin: in Inchicore and Kingstown, in Ballsbridge and Drumcondra, in Chapelizod and the Phoenix Park. The title is from 'Clay' where Joe is so moved to tears by pathetic Maria that he has to ask his wife to find the corkscrew for him, but it is clear that Joyce knew both what and where the 'corkscrew' was for each of his characters, and with dispassion and skill and humour he lays it out for all to see.

This study makes no attempt to comment on elements of style, symbol, myth or history which are not directly related to the topography of the stories. Joyce's technique, as readers of *Ulysses* know, was multi-faceted, and no one will be surprised to learn that the topographical background of his narrative is only one of the many devices he used in his art. What is surprising is the extent of the burden he assigned to place and movement and how an examination of these factors enriches our understanding of what he was about.

Map 4.18. Location of maps 4.19 (North Richmond St.); 4.20 (The Sisters: Araby); and 4.21 & 4.22 (An Encounter; Eveline). Map 4.19. North Richmond Street.

Chapter Four

NORTH RICHMOND STREET BEING BLIND

North Richmond Street

North Richmond Street where Joyce lived with his parents and nine brothers and sisters from the time he was twelve until he turned sixteen (1894-98) provided him with the imaginative setting for the first three stories in *Dubliners.* Topographical detail from these stories makes it clear that 'Araby' and 'An Encounter' begin on this street, and we may assume Joyce has the same boy and the same location for the boy's home in mind for 'The Sisters', though the emphasis in that story is on the drapery shop in nearby Great Britain Street.

North Richmond Street has one characteristic essential to Joyce's organisational design for *Dubliners:* it is a blind or dead-end street, a three-cornered box from which he can have his boy make his various attempts at escape. Each side of the street is lined with attached, tall, brick houses serving to enclose the boy even more securely within his immediate environment. The uniformly flat facades were unrelieved by any architectural deviation, and black, spiked, wrought-iron railings set in concrete separated the small, square area ways from the footpath. Three gas lamps on the east side of the street provided illumination for evening play, and an empty lot where numbers 9 and 10 had once stood allowed a rear access to Cotts Crescent and the south bank of the canal. A single, two-storey house, detached from the others in its own plot of ground, still stands at the blind end, its grounds cut off to the north and east by the Royal Canal which circles behind the street. A broader view of the city (see Map 4.18) shows how the Royal and Grand

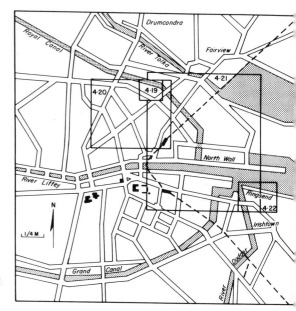

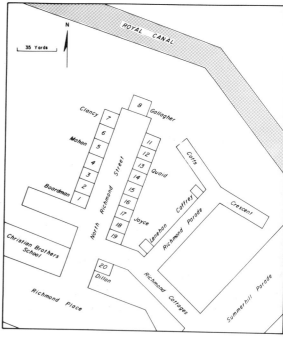

'*An uninhabited house of two storeys stood at the blind end, detached from its neighbours...*'

The North Richmond Street entrance to the Christian Brothers' School.

'*The houses, conscious of decent lives within them, gazed at one another with grown imperturbable faces.*' *North Richmond Street doorway.*

The east side of North Richmond Street.

Canals and the Rivers Tolka and Dodder tend to form 'circles' helping to entrap the citizens of Dublin. In *A Portrait of the Artist* it is Stephen's movement beyond the final circle of the Tolka that coincides with his escape from the Church, but in the early stories of *Dubliners* these water-ways serve as topographical barriers threatening to keep the characters within the paralyzing centre. To further enclose the environment, a Christian Brothers School guards the west corner of North Richmond. This school, which interrupts the quiet of the street each day when it 'sets the boys free', represents for Joyce yet another aspect of the paralyzing mechanism of life in Dublin. He and his brother Stanislaus attended this school for a few weeks in 1893 while the family was living at Millbourne Lane in Drumcondra, but by the time they moved to North Richmond Street both were enrolled at Belvedere College (see Map 4.20: ref. d).

The Joyces lived at number 17, a three-storey house on the east side of North Richmond. Like most of the other houses on the street, the residence was tall and narrow with the entry door and hall and a front parlour with its single window taking up the width of the ground floor. This parlour window looks directly across the street to where number 1 stood, the imagined residence of Mangan and his sister in 'Araby'. The kitchen was beneath the parlour in the basement, its windows giving onto the area-way in the front of the house, and if Stanislaus's memory is to be trusted, the back garden did contain the 'straggling bushes' and 'central apple tree' described in terms of a degenerate garden of Eden in 'Araby'. The back drawing-room, where according to that story the priest died, was located on the first floor above and behind the parlour, but in trying to trace the former resident of the house, we learn something which has not been reported in the various studies of Joyce's life. The city directories and tax records name John Joyce as the owner/occupant of 17 North Richmond for the years 1890-97, and since we know the family did not occupy the residence until 1894, we must assume that Joyce's father owned the house while his son was still at Clongowes Wood College and the family still at 1 Martello Terrace in Bray. Apparently, his position in the office of the Collector of Rates gave him the chance to buy the property as a rent-producing investment. If his tenant at 17 North Richmond died or left in 1894, leaving a house John Joyce owned vacant, it helps to explain why the family moved back to the city centre from Drumcondra and why it was the only residence John Joyce was able to retain for longer than a year after his fortunes began to slip and before he bought a house at 7 St Peter's Terrace in 1902 by commuting the last of his pension. As for the priest who supposedly died in the back drawing-room, that may be biographically accurate or Joyce may have been remembering Fr Quaid who disappears from number 13 North Richmond and the *Ecclesiastical Directory* in 1894 (though he is resurrected in *A Portrait of the Artist* when Stephen passes him on Bull Bridge), or he may have been thinking of Fr O'Malley who died in 1895 in nearby North William Street.

Other residents of North Richmond Street also find their way into Joyce's work. John Clancy of the sub-sheriff's office lived at number 7; he appears as Long John Fanning in *Ulysses* and under his own name in *Finnegans Wake*. Eddie and Eily Boardman, who lived across the street from Joyce, provide both Edy Boardman for *Ulysses* and Mangan and his sister for 'Araby'. Just up the street at number 20, Joe and Leo Dillon had the back garden where the boys in 'An Encounter' fight out their Indian battles, and if Mahony in that story is based on Stanislaus, as seems to be the case, the name at least is drawn from one of the Mahon boys who lived at number 5. In addition to these, there are the residents of the 'T' shaped lanes formed by Richmond Parade and Cotts Crescent located behind Joyce's house. From these he remembered the cottages, ashpits, and odorous stables for 'Araby'. Cissy Caffrey and the twins, Tommy and Jacky, lived at number 6 Richmond Parade; they appear with Edy Boardman in *Ulysses*, and from the same street at number 1, Joyce draws the character of Lenehan for 'Two Gallants'.

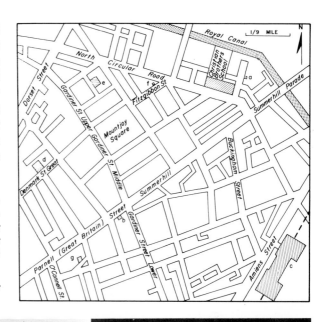

Map 4.20. 'The Sisters' of 'Araby': (a) 17 North Richmond Street, Joyce residence (1894-98); (b) The Misses Monaghan drapery; (c) Amiens Street (Connolly) Station; (d) Belvedere College; (e) Sisters of Charity Convent; (f) 14 Fitzgibbon Street, Joyce residence (1893); (g) Johnny Rush's.

Advertising posters c. 1900. Patrick's Close (Lawrence Collection, NLI).

'The Sisters' and 'Araby'

In 'The Sisters' the boy is apparently living on North Richmond Street (in keeping with the settings of 'Araby' and 'An Encounter'), perhaps at number 17 where the Joyce family lived. We learn that the drapery shop is on Great Britain Street, and Joyce seems to have the Misses Monaghan Drapery at 109 Great Britain in mind. The shop, owned by two elderly women, was situated on the south-east side of the street where it would have remained in constant shade on even the sunniest of July days. With the story's emphasis on drapery and umbrellas, it readily contrasts with 'the sunny side of the street' where the boy reads the theatrical advertisements. In Joyce's day this end of Great Britain Street was lined on both sides with shops, pro-visioners, and merchandisers and could also have served as the imaginative setting for the marketing scene in 'Araby' (see Fig. 3):

Location of the Misses Monghan drapery shop on Great Britain Street.

> We walked through the flaring streets, jostled by drunken men and bargaining women, amid the curses of labourers, the shrill litanies of shop-boys who stood guard by the barrels of pigs' cheeks, the nasal chanting of street singers. . . . These noises converged in a single sensation of life for me . . . ('Araby', p. 26).

Against all this life outside, the priest in 'The Sisters' sits in his armchair by the fire, smothered in his greatcoat or, later, lies 'solemn and copious' in his coffin.

Professor Ellmann tells us that the priest of 'The Sisters', the Rev. James Flynn, was based on a relative of Joyce's mother, and we find him, the Rev. Joseph Murray, not as parish priest at St Catherine's (as the story says) but as curate at St John the Baptist Church in Blackrock. This is the church Stephen visits with Uncle Charles in *A Portrait of the Artist* and is the church the Joyce family attended when they lived at 23 Carysfort Avenue in Blackrock in 1892. The Rev. Murray appears in the *Ecclesiastical Directory* assigned to that

GREAT BRITAIN STREET IN 1895

MARLBOROUGH STREET		GEORGE'S ST. GREAT
Pork Butcher 95		144 Wine & Spirit Mercha▪
Pork Butcher 96		143 Tallow Chandler
Boot Warehouse 97		141-2 Wine and Spirits
Grocer and Wine 98		140 Greengrocer
Colonial Meat Co. 99		139 Victualizers
		138 Bakery
CUMBERLAND LANE	G	137 Hardware and China
China & Glass Warehouse 100	R	136 Chemist
Provision Merchant 101	E	135 Dairy
Vacant 102	A	134A Greengrocer
Grocer and Wine	T	134 Tenements
Merchant 103-4		
Victualler 105	B	HILL STREET
Victualler 106	R	133 Victualler
Chandler 107	I	132 Restaurant
	T	131 Provision Dealer
CUMBERLAND STREET	A	130
Grocer 108	I	129
Drapery Shop 109	N	128
Pork Butcher 109½		127 Bakery
Druggist and Chemist 110	S	126
Poulterer 111	T	125
Tobacconist 111A	R	124
Draper 112	E	
Diningroom 113	E	BRITAIN COURT
Victualer 113A	T	
Vacant 114		123 Pharmacy
Newsagent 115		122 Hairdresser
Confectioner 116		121 Tenements
Dairy 117		120 Grocer and Bar
Grocer 118		119 Hotel and Restaurant
GARDINER STREET		GARDINER STREET

←—SUMMERHILL

church as early as 1875; he remained there until his death in 1895 (the same year, but not the same day, as Fr Flynn's death). Professor Ellmann cites Joyce's sister, Mrs May Joyce Monaghan, to the effect that the Rev. Murray 'became harmlessly insane and lost his parish' (*Joyce*, p. 19), and Joyce may be basing his story in part on some experiences he had as a child while living in Blackrock (he was ten years old in 1892). If so, he found it more appropriate for his purposes to move the story into what he considered the centre of paralysis where he could make use of the dead-end North Richmond Street and the walk west to the drapery shop.

Whatever the case, the story is not auto-biographical as regards the wake. In 1905 Joyce wrote to his brother from Trieste asking if a priest could be buried in a habit, and Stanislaus replied that 'Fr O'Malley, who had his parish taken from him, was buried in his vestments' (*Letters*, II, p. 114). Joyce follows this detail in 'The Sisters', and perhaps it is significant that Fr Thomas O'Malley, who lost his parish in 1892 and lived for his final three years near the Joyces on North William Street (see Map 4.20), is listed in the city directory next to a Mr James Flynn, who may have supplied the name for the fictitious priest in Joyce's story.

The location of the drapery shop on Great Britain Street dictates a movement

A doorway opposite Joyce's house on North Richmond Street. 'I was alone at the railways. She held one of the spikes, bowing her head towards me'.

James Joyce's residence in 1895 and the imaginative setting for 'Araby' — number 17 North Richmond Street.

for the boy which is repetitious within a clearly defined and limited area — a movement east and west between the dead-end of North Richmond Street where the boy's uncle can only advise him to 'box his corner' and the little dark room at the back of the drapery shop where Father Flynn tries to draw him into the mysteries of the priesthood. Though the boy dreams of the Eastern enchantment of Persia, there is no solace to be found in the eastward movement to his uncle's house, and the emphasis falls instead on the boy's avoiding the paralysis represented by the paralytic priest. When the boy finally refuses the eucharist-cream cracker at the wake, we feel he has momentarily evaded one of Dublin's many traps rather than having achieved any actual escape. We cannot forget that the boy's aunt has taken him back west to a house where the windows look west and reflect the false gold of the western clouds. Nor should we ignore the geometrical figure transcribed by the boy's movements as it relates to the three-sided gnomen mentioned at the beginning of the story.

Here we have yet another box being drawn which helps us to appreciate Joyce's opening sentence as it relates to the condition of the boy as well as the priest: 'There was no hope for him this time: it was the third stroke.'

There are two other topographical elements in this story which deserve attention. The distillery offers its contribution to the imagery of death with its 'faints and worms', but it also recalls the distillery where Joyce's father (here part of the character of the boy's uncle) worked as secretary in his earlier, more promising days. Its location (see Map 7.37: ref. b) in Chapelizod places Old Cotter and the uncle in close association with the dead past lying to the west. Even more obvious in its significance, the sisters report that Father Flynn had hoped to visit Irishtown (see Map. 4.18) where he had been born. It represents a

longing for the past and for youth, but it is also a destination that would have taken him eastward to the sea — a destination which, like the majority of Joyce's characters, he never achieves. Between his birth and death, the priest has moved to the west and has become paralyzed and static. He, his sisters, Old Cotter, and the aunt and uncle all offer the boy the same kind of future.

While the movement in 'The Sisters' is an oscillation between the drapery shop and North Richmond Street, the movement in 'Araby' brings the forces drawing the boy to the west and his intuitive desire toward the east into sharper conflict. In this story the boy is in quest of romance, and it is the word *Araby* and his idea of what the bazaar will be which casts 'an Eastern enchantment' over him. His plan to attend the bazaar at the Royal Dublin Society Showgrounds in Ballsbridge (see Maps 7.32 and 7.33) is opposed to his daily journey west to Belvedere College (Map 4.20: ref. d) where he finds it more and more difficult to apply himself to the 'serious work of life'. Mangan's sister, a catalyst of events in this story, continually draws the boy's attention to the west while her innocent remark about the bazaar fires his imagination and feeds his infatuation.

This girl is undoubtedly an amalgam of girls Joyce knew in his youth: Eily Boardman lived across the street from the Joyces at number 1 North Richmond where he could have watched her door from under the drawn blind of his front parlour, and Mary Sheehy, for whom Joyce 'conceived a small, rich passion' (Ellmann, p. 52), lived at 2 Belvidere Place on the corner of Fitzgibbon Street where the Joyces lived in 1893. Marvin Magalaner has suggested that she is called Mangan's sister in an allusion to the Irish poet James Clarence Mangan, and Joyce's address on that poet, delivered to the Literary and Historical Society of his college in 1902, has much about the frame of mind she induces in the boy in the story. One passage from that essay, reprinted in *The Critical Writings*, seems to bear directly on 'Araby':

> . . . any face which eyes have regarded with love . . . embody one chivalrous idea, which is no mortal thing, bearing it bravely above the accidents of lust and faithlessness and weariness; and she whose white and holy hands have the virtue of enchanted hands, his virgin flower, and flower of flowers, is no less than these an embodiment of the idea. How the East is laid under tribute for her and must bring all its treasures to her feet! (p. 79)

In this story, Mangan's sister is an embodiment of the 'chivalrous idea' for the boy, and he bears his imagined chalice bravely above the throng in the streets with her name on his lips. But she does not represent, as some commentators have suggested, all that Dublin, with its many traps, does not. She too offers the boy entrapment with the 'soft rope of her hair', and her white hands, which to the boy have the virtue of enchanted hands, focus our attention on the black spikes of the area railings which imprison the houses on this street. She draws the boy's gaze west from his parlour window and leads him west each morning as she sets out for the school attached to the Sisters of Charity Convent. The East, represented here by the Araby bazaar with its middle-eastern motif and its location south-east of North Richmond Street and towards the sea, suggests escape from the routine of Dublin life, but Mangan's sister is kept from this symbolic journey by a religious retreat in her convent.

The Sisters of Charity Convent, which the Sheehy sisters attended, is located west of Gardiner Street Upper (Map 4.20: ref. e), and Joyce apparently has this same school in mind for Mangan's sister. Thus, by setting this story on North Richmond Street and by having the boy attend Belvedere College on Great Denmark Street (ref. d),

Joyce can have his central character follow the girl west each morning until she turns north on Belvidere Place. Had he kept more strictly to autobiographical facts, he would have lost this topographical texture as well as the chance to send so young a boy so late at night on his own to the bazaar. For in May 1894, when the bazaar was actually held and when Joyce actually attended, the family was living on Millbourne Lane in Drumcondra (see Maps 3.11, 3.12, 3.13) and not on North Richmond Street where he sets the story. As the maps show, this actual location would not have allowed the west-east dichotomy between school and bazaar since all of the story's geographical elements would lie south-east of the boy's home.

Joyce himself gives us good reason to consider this departure from reality. On 5 May, 1906, he wrote to Grant Richards in defence of his book: 'I have written it [*Dubliners*] for the most part in a style of scrupulous meanness and with the conviction that he is a very bold man who dares to alter in the presentment, still more to deform, whatever he has seen and heard' (*Letters*, II, p. 134). It is a mark of Joyce's genius that he seldom found it necessary to alter the facts, so deft was he at moulding reality into art, but it is equally clear that he was ready to change the details of his and others' experience when it served his artistic purpose. Thus, the detached house in 'Araby' stands uninhabited to add to the atmosphere of the story, when in fact it was occupied by the Gallagher family during all the years Joyce lived on that street. Similarly, he takes a series of episodes and people from at least three locations he knew in his early life and structures them into the unified work of art we have in 'Araby'.

The boy in the story, about twelve years old as Joyce was in 1894, is able to make his own way to the bazaar late on its final evening by walking down Buckingham Street to the Amiens Street (Connolly)

Station (ref. c) where he takes a carriage designated for the Showgrounds. The train crosses the Liffey at Butt Bridge, turns east, passing through Westland Row (Pearse) Station, and follows a route south-east to Ballsbridge. Just as the boys in 'An Encounter' turn back west and never reach their goal, the train swings west on a spur constructed for the RDS and deposits the boy on a platform near the Merrion Road. Like many of the characters in *Dubliners*, he is ultimately disappointed and frustrated in his quest, left at the end in the darkened hall of the bazaar, his face suffused with 'anguish and anger'.

The Royal Dublin Society showgrounds buildings where the Araby Bazaar was held in May 1894.

An Encounter

Near the end of the Joyce family's first six months at 17 North Richmond Street (during Joyce's 1895 spring term at Belvedere College) Joyce and his brother Stanislaus played truant for a day, planning a journey to the Pigeonhouse Fort located out on the south wall of Dublin Bay (see Map 4.17). On the way they met and spoke with a man whom Stanislaus later characterized a 'sodomite', and this autobiographical episode became the basis for the story 'An Encounter'. Once again Joyce is able to use Belvedere College to the west to represent the 'weariness of school-life' while dead-end North Richmond Street can offer only the equally tiresome 'mimic warfare of the evening' which ironically serves as a training-ground for the priesthood. In search of real adventure, the boy is drawn to the east, to the sea, and to the fort with its associations nautical, military and spiritual. So his plans are laid: he is to meet Mahony and Dillon in the morning at Newcomen Bridge; they will cross the Liffey by ferry-boat and walk the mile and a half along the south wall to the Pigeonhouse.

The Pigeonhouse was soon (1897) to become the site of the Dublin Corporation electric power station, but at the time this story takes place the fort was a derelict but evocative setting for a day's adventure. Originally the port authorities had built a large, iron-reinforced, wooden structure on the site in order to provide a watch tower for the harbour and a store house which would double as a shelter for sea-tossed travellers. The caretaker, a man named Pidgeon, took advantage of the interest generated during the construction and developed the place into a kind of road-house. It became not only the resort of travellers but a favourite haunt of many of Dublin's distinguished citizens, wits and wags. It soon became known as Pidgeon's House or the Pigeonhouse, and when a passenger station was established there in the eighteenth century for those arriving from or leaving for Liverpool, it was called the Pigeonhouse Packet Station and its harbour and newly built hotel went by that name as well. Stories, current in Dublin during Joyce's childhood, told of the pit-falls, bandits (freelance and official Government Customs both), press-gangs and rebels which made the journey between the city and the packet station more exciting than many might have wished. These may be reflected in Mahony's coming armed (with catapult).

The passenger services on the south wall were eventually superseded by the packet facilities at Howth, and in 1813 the government bought the station and hotel and, using the latter as the centre of its fortifications, began construction of the Pigeonhouse Fort. This fort, built to defend the port of Dublin and to serve as an emergency repository for State papers and valuables, boasted a submarine mining operation and a string of formidable batteries, several of which were trained on the passage along the south wall rather than upon the harbour. This led Weston St John Joyce to suggest that the authorities were more apprehensive of an Irish attack from land than of a foreign attack from sea, and Joyce could have had this in mind as another symbolic physical barrier to the boy's escape. St John Joyce's handbook, *The Neighbourhood of Dublin* (1912), issued in part in earlier versions in Dublin newspapers of the 1880's and 1890's and in *Rambles Round Dublin* (1887) and *Rambles Near Dublin* (1890), also has a photograph of the entrance to the Pigeonhouse Fort (p. 8) taken in the same year Joyce and Stanislaus attempted their abortive journey; it shows a barricade of sharpened wooden posts and a sentry at attention before a very British-looking guardhouse.

Thus, as Joyce has the boys set out from North Richmond Street in the story, their destination is multi-suggestive, calling up both an embarkation point for England and the Continent and a final barricade to keep

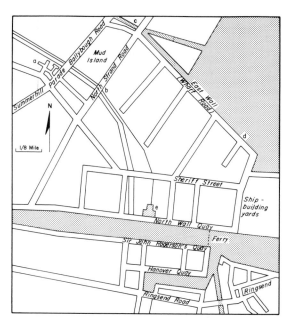

The ruins of the Pigeon House Fort near the Dublin electric power station on Pigeon House Road.

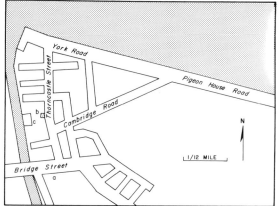

Map 4.21. 'An Encounter' and 'Eveline: (a) North Richmond St; (b) Newcomen Bridge; (c) Vitriol works; (d) Smoothing iron; (e) North Wall Station.

Map 4.22. 'An Encounter': (a) Grocery in Ringsend; (b) Huckster's shop in Ringsend; (c) Empty fields overlooking the Dodder river.

Two boys, away from school for the day, pass beneath the Ballybough Bridge as they follow the canal to North Strand Road.

them in place. Its name (and Mahony's wish to 'have some gas with the birds') remind us of the holy spirit who visited Mary in the form of a dove, lending a layer of spiritual significance to the destination and reinforcing the contrast with Fr Butler and the other Jesuits of Belvedere College.

Since North Richmond Street backs onto the Royal Canal, the boy's shortest route to the meeting place at Newcomen Bridge is to follow the canal bank walk which passes under the bridge at Summerhill Parade, runs along beside Charleville Mall, and emerges at North Strand Road. He hides his school books at the back of the garden behind his house (Joyce probably imagines number 17 North Richmond), and he can easily reach the canal behind Cotts Crescent (see Map 4.19). Mahony has planned some other subterfuge to avoid his parents' scrutiny: perhaps he sets off west toward Belvedere College and circles around to approach the rendezvous from the south. In the story, the boy sees him coming up the hill of the North Strand Road from his vantage point on the granite coping of the bridge (Map 4.21: ref. b).

Leo Dillon's failure to appear leaves his sixpence forfeit, and splitting his share of the money, the two boys head north on North Strand Road making for Annesley Bridge and Wharf (now East Wall) Road. Their route takes them past the once-notorious Mud Island. Legend had it that three brothers, driven from their ancestral lands at the time of the Plantation of Ulster, came to Dublin, one of them settling on a tract of waste ground by the sea. Joyce may have known of the area from St John Joyce's *Rambles Near Dublin* (1890):

Westward of the North Strand, between Nottingham Street and Newcomen Bridge, and extending as far as Ballybough Road, was a locality of evil repute in former times, known as Mud Island, inhabited by a gang of smugglers, high-waymen, and desperadoes of every

description, and ruled by a hereditary robber chief rejoicing in the title of 'King of Mud Island'. For about 200 years down to the middle of the last century, this den of robbers was a plague spot in the district, enjoying an extra-ordinary immunity from molestation in consequence of what had at length come to be regarded as a sort of prescriptive right and sanctuary attaching to the locality, until at last no officer of the law durst show his nose within its sacred precincts . . . (p. 244).

In 'An Encounter' the stone-throwing boys and failed siege serve as the historical analogue and help to reinforce the feeling of heightened adventure which pervades the first part of the story.

The first suggestion that decay and degeneracy will become a central aspect of the story as well is introduced when Joyce mentions the Vitriol Works as the boys approach Annesley Bridge. This manufac-turing plant belonged to the Dublin and Wicklow Manure Company. Once a flint-glass factory where fine plate glass was fashioned for the coaches of the ascen-dency, the plant now extracted liquid bleach from rotted manure. The aura of decay its suggests eventually comes to dominate the story as the day grows sultry and the boys' resolve to reach the Pigeon-house fades. The Tolka sloblands, the musty biscuits and chocolate, the squalid neighbourhood of Ringsend, the empty field overlooking the sewage-filled Dodder, and, most notably, the pervert in his ashen-grey moustache and greenish-black suit — these all belong to this line of imagery.

The boys arrange their failed siege at the Smoothing Iron (Map 4.21: ref. d), a bathing-place which once existed at the end of Merchants' Road, so-called because a diving-stone here suggested the shape of an old-fashioned pressing-iron. They then con-tinue along Wharf Road spending a long time walking about the 'noisy streets flank-

ed by high stone walls.' These were the
ship-building yards and areas of port commerce east of North Wall Quay. The area is
described rather proudly in Dillon Cosgrave's
study of North Dublin (1909):

> The North Wall Extension, dating from
> 1875, and since enlarged, contains berth-
> age for the biggest fourmasters; also the
> new and fine Alexandria Basin, called
> after the present Queen, which could
> hold all the old Docks; and, best of all,
> for Dublin, the prosperous ship-building
> yard of the Dublin Dockyard and Com-
> pany, established a few years ago. . . .
> The Graving Dock, Customs Watch
> House, and Hundred Ton Crane are also
> features of the Extension (p. 74).

It is noon by the time the boys tear
themselves away from this spectacle and
reach the North Wall Quay bordering the
Liffey. After lunching on currant buns
purchased on the quay and watching a
sailing vessel being unloaded across the
river on Sir John Rogerson's Quay, they
cross the Liffey on one of the four ferry-
boats then offering service to the south
wall for a uniform fare of ½d. Their walk
becomes more desultory as they wander
into Ringsend, crossing the Grand Canal via
the wooden plank walkway provided by
the triple set of locks at the end of Britain
Quay (Map 4.21: ref. f). From here a path
runs along beside the Dodder giving access
to Ringsend Road Bridge as well as a view
of the empty field on the opposite bank
where their journey will end. The grocers'
shops where the musty biscuits lay bleaching in the windows were located in a row at
numbers 4, 8 and 14 Bridge Street (Map
4.22: ref. a), and after buying some biscuits
and chocolate from one of these shops the
boys turn left into Thorncastle Street, still
heading for Pigeon House Road and their
destination. Joyce is accurate when he remembers that there was no dairy in this
neighbourhood and right, too, when he
recalls the huckster's shop that William

Grimley kept at 39 Thorncastle between
Commercial Court and Whiskey Row (Map
4.22: ref. b). Mahony chases a cat down
the lane near this shop and the boys find
themselves in an empty field overlooking
the Dodder River (Map 4.22: ref. c). This
abrupt turn to the west into a waste ground
serves as a symbol of the failure of their
quest, and Ringsend with its dilapidated
and grimy houses, its grease manufacturers
and chemical manure factories, serves as an
appropriate setting for the confrontation
with the pervert.

*'We spent a long time walking about the noisy streets,
watching the workings of cranes and engines' ('An Encounter').*

Richmond Avenue. 'Then a man from Belfast built houses — not like their little brown houses, but bright brick houses with shining roofs.'

Title page of Irish Homestead *(courtesy NLI) in which 'Eveline' was published in Sept. 1904, one month before Joyce left Ireland with Nora Barnacle to begin his self-imposed exile.*

The North Wall Station from Sir John Rodgerson's Quay, across the Liffey.

Eveline

Richard Ellmann identifies Eveline Thornton as the model for Eveline Hill in this story, and he cites Joyce's sister, Mrs May Monaghan, to the effect that the Thornton family lived across the street from the Joyces on North Richmond Street in the city. This creates a problem in assessing Joyce's use of the Dublin he knew because the description in 'Eveline' is definitely not a description of North Richmond Street where his first three stories take place:

> She sat at the window watching the evening invade the avenue. . . . Few people passed. The man out of the last house passed on his way home; she heard his footsteps clacking along the concrete pavement and afterwards crunching on the cinder path before the new red houses. One time there used to be a field in which they used to play every evening with other people's children. Then a man from Belfast bought the field and built houses in it — not like their little brown houses, but bright brick houses with shining roofs. The children of the avenue used to play together in that field — the Devines, the Waters, the Dunns, little Keogh the cripple, she and her brothers and sisters ('Eveline', p. 32).

This would not be a difficulty with most writers, but it has become clear that Joyce grounded his stories in reality, using real people and, for the most part, scrupulously accurate detail in his creation of setting. Would Joyce, who so assiduously verified the details for his stories (see *Letters*, II, pp. 109, 192-3), choose a setting for 'Eveline' so at odds with what he had known? If so, it would suggest he had an overriding structural or imagistic purpose and, for this story only, radically altered his working technique. In fact, May Joyce, who was only four years old when the family moved to North Richmond Street, has apparently confused the location of the

Thorntons with a later address the Joyces occupied.

Stanislaus Joyce tells us in *My Brother's Keeper* that in April 1900 the family was living in Fairview in 'a house with many spacious rooms, gates and a garden, or rather a neglected field large enough for me and my school friends to play football in, five or six to a side', (p. 107). He refers here to the house at 13 Richmond Avenue, the second of three the Joyces occupied between 1898 and 1901 (see Map 3.16: ref. b). This neighbourhood lies just about a half-mile north-east of North Richmond Street and just beyond the 'circle' defined by the Tolka River; as such, it serves symbolically as a fitting location for 'Eveline' wherein the central character is denied escape not by her environment but by something within herself. In Fairview Eveline is not held to the centre of paralysis by topographical barriers as the boy in the earlier stories is. The very name suggests a clear view of the sea and the escape it represents, and it is a short journey on the map of Dublin to the North Wall Station (Map 4.21: ref. e) where she is to leave for a new life with Frank. It is a journey, however, which she is psychologically unable to complete.

There is no doubt Joyce has the Fairview address in mind as the imaginative setting for this story. Eveline Thornton lived across the street from the Joyces at number 42 Richmond Avenue, the Keoghs of the story were four doors below the Joyce home at number 9, 'Tizzie' Dunn and her parents lived on the avenue as well in a row of terraced houses at number 2, and the Waters were nearby at number 6 Melrose. The empty lot which both Joyce's brother and Eveline remember was at the head of the avenue at number 31 before the 'bright brick houses' came to fill the field.

Hugh Kenner identifies Frank in this story with Joyce, basing his deduction in part on the C.P. Curran photograph of Joyce in 1904 (*The Pound Era,* pp.35-6), and, of course, Joyce did persuade Nora to leave with him 'for a new life' from the same North Wall Station where Eveline stands paralyzed. In order to keep the truth from his father, Joyce boarded the ship first as if he were leaving alone, and Professor Ellmann suggests that 'the possibility that Nora might change her mind at the last moment, like the girl of his story "Eveline", must have been in his thought' (p. 185). This departure was in October 1904, and Joyce had published 'Eveline' the previous month in the *Irish Homestead.* It seems likely that he may have been thinking of leaving with Nora when he wrote the story, and Nora's sister has noted that Nora thought that Joyce, with his yachting cap, was a sailor when she first met him (Ellmann, p. 162). But Eveline's character and circumstances in this story do not fit the situation in which Nora found herself at the time of Joyce's proposal. She is described as witty and spirited, jaunty and daring (the antithesis of what we see in Eveline), and she had left her uncle's house in Galway at the beginning of 1904 and was living on her own at Finn's Hotel with little if anything to tie her to the city of Dublin. A more likely candidate to have added to the characterization initiated by Eveline Thornton (Eveline did marry a sailor but settled with him in Dublin) was Joyce's sister, Margaret. Born in 1884, she would have been twenty years old when this story was written. Joyce's mother had died eighteen months earlier, and it was left to Margaret to act as mother and housekeeper for the family and to talk her father out of what shillings she could in order to put food on the table. It was also, according to Stanislaus, the Joyce family who often went to the Hill of Howth for a day's picnic when their mother was alive and the family lived in Fairview.

Chapter 5

FIFTY-SIX WHISKEYS

Two Gallants

As can be seen on Map 5.24, the quality of the movement in 'Two Gallants' is repetitive, circular, and wandering — characteristics which reflect the lives of the two central characters. We follow Lenehan for two hours as he passes the time waiting for Corley's return from Donnybrook. He walks aimlessly around the city centre, retracing his steps and describing three complete circles to end back where he begins. Without setting his walk on the map of Dublin, however, the circular nature of his wandering is easily lost on the reader unfamiliar with the city.

Lenehan and Corley are introduced as they come down the hill of Rutland (Parnell) Square. Lenehan has spent the afternoon in a pub on Dorset Street, perhaps either Larry O'Rourke's on the corner of Eccles Street or Thomas M'Auley's further along Dorset Street (see Map 5.27: refs. b and c). The two gallants proceed down Sackville Street and into College Green, Lenehan skipping out into the street to see the clock on the front of Trinity College. They follow the railings of the college around into Nassau Street and turn south into Kildare Street, passing the Protestant-Unionist Kildare Street Club (ref. b) where they see the harpist playing to 'a little ring of listeners'. Crossing the street to Stephen's Green, Corley goes on ahead to meet the girl who waits at the corner of Hume Street. Lenehan follows at a discrete distance, watching as Corley and the girl enter a tram at the corner of Merrion Square and Clare Street.

Lenehan, faced with the problem of killing time until Corley returns from the empty field in Donnybrook (see Map 4.17), can think of nothing but to keep walking. He backtracks down Merrion Street, circles Stephen's Green, and, going down Grafton Street, returns to Rutland Square. After spending some time in a refreshment bar on Great Britain Street (ref. g), he heads back for Grafton Street along Capel, George's, Exchequer and Wicklow Streets. From here he returns once again to Stephen's Green and walks along the west side of the Green far enough to be able to check the clock on the front of the College of Surgeons (ref. a) then retraces his steps and proceeds down the north side of the Green.

He waits at the corner of Merrion and Baggot Streets, and after Corley has returned and duly received the gold coin from the girl, the two gallants turn into the cul-de-sac of Ely Place, ending up appropriately enough in front of the Valuer's Office at number 6 Ely Place as they stop under the first street lamp to examine the symbol of Corley's conquest. The whole walk, in terms of places called to mind and quality of movement, serves to emphasize the false gallantry of the central characters and to subtly comment on lives without meaning or direction.

Throughout this story, Joyce emphasizes circles, calling our attention immediately to the warm air and swarming crowds circulating in the streets and then to at least thirty circular images including the 'pale disk' of the moor 'circled in a double halo', the round plate of round peas, and the small gold coin finally revealed in the round palm of Corley's hand. In keeping with the aimless circling of the characters' lives, clocks

College Green, Dublin (Lawrence Collection NLI). 'As they passed along the railways of Trinity College, Lenehan skipped out into the road and peered up at the clock.'

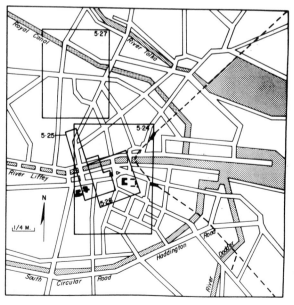

Map 5.23. Showing location of maps 5.24, ('Two Gallants'); 5.25 ('A Little Cloud'); 5.26 ('Counterparts'); 5.27 ('Grace').

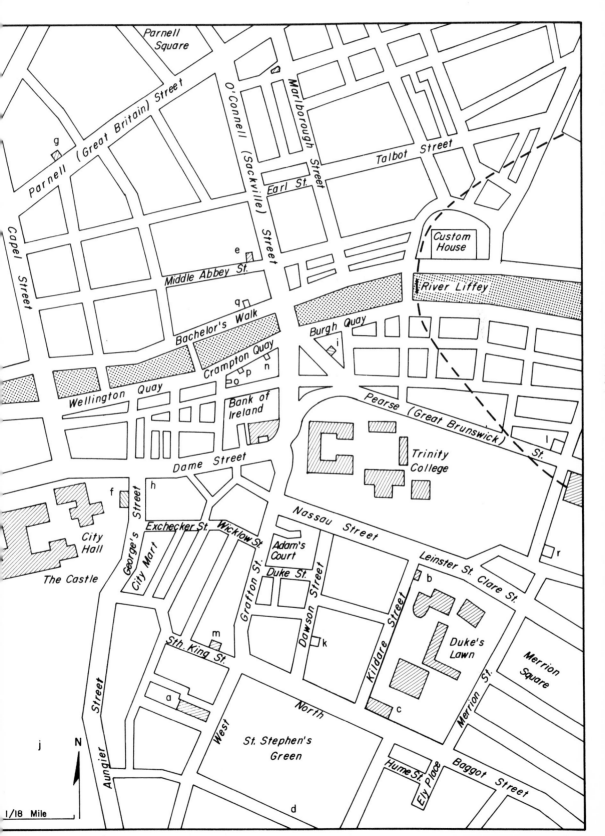

appear prominently in the story as Lenehan worries about the time. Besides the clocks on Trinity College and the College of Surgeons, Corley tells us that he first met the girl under Waterhouse's clock (the letters 'H. Waterhouses' replaced the numerals on the dial), and the friends Lenehan meets on the corner of George's Street make reference not only to billiard balls and to Egan's pub (it was called the 'Oval') but to Westmoreland Street, calling up the clock and famous time ball on the Ballast Office, one of the most conspicuous features of the street. In addition, the two characters are described, both physically and in terms of personality, in relation to circles: 'rotund' Lenehan standing on the edge of the circle in a pub until he is included in a round, Corely with his 'globular' head like a 'big ball revolving on a pivot'. It is not surprising that the movement in the story develops and reinforces this circular imagery, and that for all the walking neither character really gets anywhere.

Lenehan's walk describes three complete circles, one around Stephen's Green, one bounded by Grafton, Nassau, Kildare and Stephen's Green North, and the large circle formed by Sackville, Great Britain and Capel Streets on the east, north and west and by Dame, Exchequer and Wicklow Streets on the south. Our notice is also called to the 'circles' of Merrion Square, the Trinity College grounds, and Rutland Square (with its Rotunda), as well as the smaller 'circle' formed by the Duke's Lawn opposite Merrion Square.

Map 5.24: 'Two Gallants': (a) College of Surgeons; (b) Kildare Street Club; (c) Shelbourne Hotel; (d) The chains around Stephen's Green; (e) Egan's 'Oval' Pub; (f) Pim's; (g) 'refreshment bar'; (h) Waterhouse's Clock; (i) Irish Times ('Grace'); (j) Jacob's Biscuit Factory (A Portrait); (k) Mansion House ('Ivy Day'); (l) Antient Concert Rooms ('A Mother'); (m) Gaiety Theatre ('The Dead'); (n) Webb's ('The Dead'); (o) O'Clohissey's ('The Dead'); (p) Massey's ('The Dead'); (q) Hickey's ('The Dead'); (r) Academy of Music ('The Dead');

Corley and the girl play their part in this development as well, returning again to the empty, 'circular' waste ground south of the city and then circling back to the city centre by tram. The thrust of Joyce's point is made, however, when he has Lenehan and Corley walk into Ely Place at the conclusion of the story. Not only does it suggest the dead-end of their lives, but it means that the two characters must either retrace their steps once again or exit via Hume Street, thereby completing yet another circle as they begin to make their way back across the city.

Donald Torchiana has written a long article for the *James Joyce Quarterly* (VI, 2: 1968) wherein he details what he sees as Joyce's use in this story of multiple topographical allusions to the debauchery, perfidy and false nobility of eighteen-century Dublin's garrison community. From Rutland Square to Stephen's Green, from Trinity College to Pim's, from Sackville Street to the South Circular Road, he notes the historical associations he finds as these correspond to what he calls 'the decadent commingling of greed, peremptory self-righteousness, and sexual intrigue apparent virtually from the story's exceedingly balmy beginning' (p. 117).

Thus he begins by calling our attention to the Kildare Street Club where the harp, 'her coverings . . . fallen about her knees', represents a debased and weary Irish nationality offering its weary song before the porch of a club whose membership, according to Torchiana, 'epitomized the religious, social, and economic callousness' (p. 116) of the English in eighteenth-century Dublin. This article then goes on to note that, throughout 'Two Gallants', the 'litany of streets and places is one of almost unrelievedly black hints of betrayal and extravagance repeated at every turn Corley and Lenehan make' (p. 117). The list of betrayers associated with place includes Rutland Square, calling to mind the Orange Lodge which first occupied the grounds, the

Above: *A tram on Stephen's Green. Photo shows the College of Surgeons colonnaded facade. (Lawrence Collection, NLI).* Left: *The Ballast Office clock in Westmoreland Street.* Overleaf: *'Lehehan said that he had been with Mac the night before in Egan's.' — Egan's Oval Pub in Henry Street Middle, though not visited by the 'Two Gallants', serves to reinforce the circular imagery of the story.*

notorious General Henry Lawes Luttrell, and the turncoat Frederick Jebb, Master of the Rotunda Hospital; Nassau Street, directly associated with William of Orange; Sackville Street, a 'thoroughfare of near treachery and royal reward' (p. 119) in the person of Lord George Sackville; Earl Street (Earl of Meath), Hume Street (Gustavus Hume) and Ely Place (Lord Ely) all suggesting the extravagance of those who 'erected their palatial residences on profits exacted from an oppressed tenantry' (p. 121); and Grafton Street, associated with Henry Fitzroy who deserted James II in favour of William III in 1689. Stephen's Green with its Beaux's Walk is the 'centre of gallantry' (p. 121), the Shelbourne Hotel on the north side of the Green is a former British barracks housing troops who had come to put down the rebellion of 1798, and even the clocks in the story are found 'tinted with betrayal and coercion' (p. 123), representing as they do bastions of Protestant-Unionist influence and intrigue.

Beyond these, Torchiana finds the references to financial matters equally compelling. In keeping with Corley's quest for the gold half-sovereign, we are reminded that Frederick Jebb was paid by the Lord Lieutenant to change his politics and write in favour of the Act of Union, that Lord Ely, like others of his class, accepted a £30,000 bribe to vote for that Union, that Capel Street where Lenehan walks, concern-

ed about Corley's success, was the site of the King James Mint-House, that City Hall at the end of the street was once the Royal Exchange, and that even the lane where Lenahan turns at the City Markets was named after a banker. Though Torchiana goes too far at times in his search for significance, he has clearly revealed that Joyce brings his modern gallants along a route where self-serving finance and ascendancy betrayal and moral dissipation come together to make their unstated comment on the evening's activities.

There are several other topographical details which today's reader might find interesting. Waterhouse's, where Corley meets the Baggot Street slavey for the first time, is listed in *Thom's Directory* for 1900 as 'Gold and Silversmiths . . . to His Majesty and the Irish Court', a reference appropriate to the central concern of all the characters in the story. Earl Street, mentioned in reference to the fall into prostitution of the girl from the South Circular Road, is cited in John Finegan's *The Story of Monto* as the primary entrance to Dublin's red-light district. Finegan tells of the pony traps which would carry the girls in their finery to the Horse Show at Ballsbridge, for example, and of how, having aroused the passions of their would-be customers, 'a clatter of cabs and outside cars would pursue the pony traps back to Monto, dashing along Earl and Talbot Streets from Sack-

ville Street to the Mabbot Street entrance to the Irish Walpurgisnacht' (p. 12). The South-Circular girl in this story has been seen on a jaunting car with two men in this street, and there can be no doubt of her destination or her new profession. Finally, something should be said about the suburb of Donnybrook which Corley chooses as the site of his conquest. In discussing the famous Donnybrook Fair, Weston St John Joyce (*The Neighbourhood of Dublin*) tells us that by 1906 few realized that the 'deserted, low-lying field on the left as we pass out of the village is the historic ground where for over six-hundred years was held the world-renowned Fair of Donnybrook, so famed for fighting, dancing, lovemaking, and drollery, and so long associated with the name and character of the Irish people' (p. 76). But Joyce must have been well aware of this fact when he wrote 'Two Gallants', for it is clear that he has Corley destined for this same deserted field lying on the north side of Donnybrook Road just beyond what is today Eglington Terrace. Like the waste ground in 'An Encounter', this field overlooks the River Dodder, and as old maps of the district show, it was the only likely place in Donnybrook for the kind of assignation Corley has in mind. By the turn-of-the-century, Donnybrook had become a respectable neighbourhood of quiet homes and shops, the residents anxious to wipe out the memory of the annual summer Bacchanal which had graced and disgraced their suburb for over six hundred years. The fair, established by Royal Charter in 1204, took place each year in August (as do the events of 'Two Gallants'), until public subscription raised the funds to purchase the patent and put an end to what Weston Joyce characterizes a 'gigantic public nuisance and disgrace' (p. 76). Most historians agree with his assessment, F. Elrington Ball (*History of the County Dublin*, 1903) calling the fair an 'occasion of drunkness, riot, and moral degradation . . . a disgrace

to Ireland', and its abolition 'a service to civilization' (rpt. in Torchiana, p. 120). But it is the moral degradation associated with the field in Donnybrook which Joyce wishes us to remember, for in the final analysis this story plots the rejection and degradation of true gallantry in a Dublin where one character, at least, has been trapped in a life of aimless watching and waiting and wandering while the other can achieve only a debased conquest of his own honour.

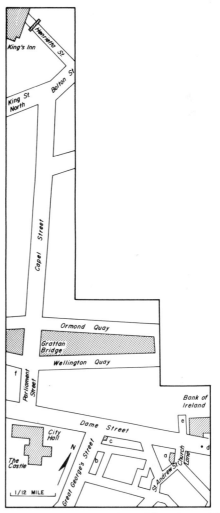

Map 5.25: 'A Little Cloud' (a) Corless's; (b) Bewley's; (c) Eating house in George's Street ('A Painful Case'); (d) King Billy's statue ('The Dead'); (e) Foster Place (A Portrait); (f) Kavanagh's ('Ivy Day').

Top: *'He emerged from under the feudal arch of the King's Inns and walked swiftly down Henrietta Street.* Below: *A doorway on decaying Henrietta Street 'under the shadow of the gaunt spectral mansions in which the old nobility of Dublins had roistered.'*

A Little Cloud

The movement in 'A Little Cloud' is straightforward, yet there are elements of the topography which lend depth to our understanding of the central character and his predicament. Little Chandler travels from the King's Inns to a degree of self-realization, disillusioned by the vulgarity he observes in Ignatius Gallaher and finally brought to remorse for his futile life as he sees the hatred in his wife's eyes. In a way, the streets through which he walks are an analogue for the fate he will inevitably suffer.

Little Chandler works as a clerk in the King's Inns at a desk which overlooks the ordered lawns and formal gardens facing Constitution Hill (see Map 2.10). Though he likes to gaze in this direction from his tiresome copy work, the life in which he feels trapped is more in keeping with the rear entrance through the 'feudal arch' to Henrietta Street. The *Dictionary of Dublin* (1906) calls this entrance to the Inns 'prison-like and depressing', and it undoubtedly had this same effect on Little Chandler as he passed out from under it each day into the depression of Henrietta Street. There he is continually reminded of how useless it is to struggle against fate. The Gardiner family had once resided on Henrietta Street, as had the Earls of Blessington and the Viscounts Mountjoy, but at the time of the story it was populated with a 'horde of grimy children' who 'squatted like mice upon the thresholds' of the decaying houses. If Little Chandler had once taken solace from the grandeur of Dublin's past, the houses he passes each afternoon in the 'waning sunset' forebode the years ahead and make his meeting with Gallaher on this day all the more urgent.

From Henrietta Street, he turns south into Bolton Street and walks down Capel Street, once the most fashionable promanade of the city and a popular residential location. On this day, however, his soul revolts against the 'dull inelegance' into

'As he crossed Grattan Bridge he looked down the river towards the lower quays and pitied the poor stunted houses' Grattan Bridge (Lawrence Collection, NLI).

which the street had fallen, and we can not help but feel that his own character, carefully groomed with an old-fashioned refinement, will settle into a similar inelegance as he remains in Dublin. He pauses on Grattan Bridge to gaze eastward towards the lower quays and the 'poor stunted houses' huddled there, and we would probably be right to imagine that he is staring with self-pity at his own home at that very time. The Bewley's his wife expects him to pass on his way home is located on George's Street (ref. b), and his journey this evening seems to be the way he always goes home from work. He absent-mindedly walks past Church Street and has to retrace his steps as if it was his habit to pass this way regularly, and he speaks of often walking past Corless's at night, perhaps after a parcel of coffee or tea for his wife.

Little Chandler's walk has taken him from the King's Inn to Corless's Restaurant (ref. a) on the corner of Church Lane and St Andrew's Street, these two termini suggesting an allegorical journey through life and perhaps a crucifixion such as St Andrew suffered on the cross of Irish family life. It may be coincidental that this story takes place in late autumn when St Andrew's feast day is celebrated on November 30, and it may indeed be stretching matters to note that his trip from work to restaurant describes an X-shaped cross as he passes over the River Liffey, the same cross saltire on which St Andrew was crucified and which now serves as his emblem. But it seems beyond coincidence to find the two central characters on St Andrew's Street with names which suggest two well-known saints, particularly when Ignatius Gallaher acts as the 'teacher' (St Ignatius founded the Jesuits, a teaching Order) and Thomas Chandler takes the role of apostle to Gallaher's continental sophistication, demanding from Gallaher what St Thomas demanded of Christ: proof that he was 'the way, the truth, and the life' (John xiv, 5-7).

In relation to Chandler's name and the line of thought suggested by St Andrew's Street, it is interesting to note that St Thomas More, known best as the author of *Utopia*, travelled in his life from Lincoln's Inn (where he studied law) to Parliament, was married, became Lord Chancellor of England, was imprisoned and then executed when his religious beliefs displeased Henry VIII. There is a similar movement here as Chandler travels from King's Inns on Henrietta Street, down Capel Street (recalling Arthur Capel, Lord Lieutenant in Ireland) into Parliament Street, east into Dame Street, and thus to his own growing recognition of imprisonment and defeat on Church Lane. Also, as he crosses Grattan Bridge and walks toward Dublin Castle, he just skirts the old Liberties of the Abbey of St Thomas à Becket, another St Thomas who moved from the king's realm (Henry II) to the Church's. Joyce with his strong Jesuit education would have been aware of these points and was probably pleased to see the correspondences piling up almost without his having to lift a finger.

The way the talk in Corless's turns to the immorality of London and continental Europe, the information that Ignatius Gallaher was 'wild' in his youth (as St Ignatius was before his conversion), the fact that Gallaher is now in a position to reveal 'many of the secrets of religious houses on the Continent', Gallaher's interest in Paris where St Ignatius first brought the incipient Jesuits together, his disparaging comments on marriage (in favour of sexual variety) compared to St Ignatius's vow of celibacy — all of these may have grown out of the St Andrew/St Thomas/St Ignatius line of development. In the end, Little Chandler, who has only been to the Isle of Man, is disabused of his romantic idealization of the Continent by Gallaher's coarse stories, and this is the real point of what happens in the restaurant. But though he recognizes that Gallaher's 'mere tawdry journalism' cannot compare to what he

Dame Street looking towards Trinity College. Eustace Street and the the office of Crosbie and Alleyne are on the left. (Lawrence, NLI)

could accomplish, he also recognizes that his unfortunate timidity forbids his entering into Gallaher's 'vagrant and triumphant life', and the ambience of the bar where he comes to this recognition emphasizes the contrast between the life he lives and the life he wishes.

The Burlington Hotel at 26-27 St Andrew's Street and 6 Church Lane was owned and operated until 1903 by Thomas Corless, and the restaurant and bar attached to the premises is variously characterized in *Thom's Directory* during these years as 'dining rooms', 'oyster saloons' and an 'oyster house'. Stephen Dedalus calls it 'Underdone's' in *A Portrait,* where we get the impression that it has not yet become the impressive oasis of cosmopolitan glamour it seems to be in 'A Little Cloud'. Stephen has just cashed his exhibition prizes at the Bank of Ireland and joined his family on the corner of Foster Place across the street from the restaurant:

> — We had better go to dinner, said Stephen. Where?
> — Dinner? said Mr Dedalus. Well I suppose we had better, what?
> — Some place that's not too dear, said Mrs Dedalus.
> — Underdone's?
> — Yes, some quiet place.
> — Come along, said Stephen quickly. It doesn't matter about the dearness.
> *(A Portrait,* p. 97)

This episode is based on events which took place in 1897, but by 1905, when 'A Little Cloud' was completed, the Burlington Hotel had been purchased by the Jammett Brothers who turned it into a cosmopolitan, gourmet restaurant specializing in French cuisine. This is the restaurant Joyce has in mind for this story. The initial brightness and gaiety of the red and green glasses mingle in Chandler's imagination with thoughts of the Moulin Rouge and the Bohemian cafés of Paris, but he and the reader are both quickly reminded that the

excitement these represent are not for a 'pious chap' like Little Chandler. We imagine he would feel more at ease in 'Underdone's' Oyster House, while the life he wants but can not muster the courage to grasp is represented in this story by Jammetts' 'High-Class French Restaurant'. Right at the start when we see him indecisive and agitated by the light and noise at the door of the bar, we can guess that we will not escape from 'old jog-along Dublin', and soon the colour and brightness he finds in this momentary refuge are replaced by the reality of hire-purchase furniture and a crying child. Faced with his wife's contempt, he steps 'back out of the lamplight', resigned to a life of imprisonment and remorse.

Joyce probably would have been pleased to learn that many years later, Jammett's Restaurant moved to Nassau Street to make room for an expanding Bank of Ulster where it took over the premises of the Empire Buffet. This latter public house finds its way into *Dubliners* as well as *Ulysses*, as does Jammett's, and reinforces Joyce's contention that all places were the same place — that the particular yields the universal.

Top left: *'From the street he walked on furtively on the inner side of the path'* — *Eustace St. from O'Neill's pub looking towards Dame St.*

Top centre: *'He was now safe in the dark snug of O'Neill's shop.'*

Top right: *Davy Byrne's at 21 Duke Street.*

Left: *The Scotch House* — *'the bar was full of men and loud with the noise of tongues and glasses.'*

Centre right: *'When the Scotch House closed they went round to Mulligan's.*

Bottom right: *'His tram let him down at Shellbourne Road and he steered his great body along in the shadow of the wall of the barracks' at Beggar's Bush.*

Counterparts

In the mid-1890s John Joyce worked occasionally for a solicitor named Aylward in an office located on the Liffey quays, and Professor Ellmann (*James Joyce*, p. 39) suggests that this office, under the name of Crosbie and Alleyne, became the starting point for Farrington in 'Counterparts'. His argument is that Joyce changed the name of the solicitor to Alleyne in order to get revenge for his father at the expense of one Henry Alleyne. This latter Alleyne had embezzled funds from the Dublin and Chapelizod Distilling Company (see Map 7.37) in the late 1870s, funds which included £500 John Joyce had put into the business. Though Joyce may have had Henry Alleyne in mind as well, he clearly starts Farrington on his 'pub crawl' from Dame Street, and Joyce would have known of C.W. Alleyne, a solicitor practising at 24 Dame Street near the corner of Great George's Street South and of Collis and Ward, Solicitors, a few doors down at 31 Dame Street. It seems that he creates the fictitious Crosbie and Alleyne from these two concerns and sets their office on the corner of Dame and Eustace Streets (ref. a). Farrington himself is an amalgam of Joyce's father and his uncle, William Murray. Murray lived for a time at 16 Shelbourne Road, Farrington's destination as he steers for home (see Map 3.16: ref. j), and he worked as a billing-clerk ('drunken little costdrawer', Simon Dedalus calls him in *Ulysses*) for the firm of Collis and Ward mentioned above. Stanislaus Joyce's diary reports that it was Murray's son, Bertie, who actually said, 'I'll say a "Hail Mary" for you, pa, if you don't beat me', and the whole family appears in *Ulysses* disguised under the name of Goulding.

The quality of the movement in this story reminds the reader of Lenehan's walk in 'Two Gallants', especially in its repetitive character. Farrington slips out of the office and down Eustace Street to the 'dark snug of O'Neill's shop', a small bar owned at the time by J.J. O'Neill at the corner of Eustace and Essex Street East (ref.: b). He then returns to the office and, after suffering the first of several public humiliations, goes back down Eustace and past O'Neill's on his way to the alley of Temple Bar and to Terry Kelly's Pawn Office at 48 Fleet Street (ref. c). He emerges in Westmoreland Street with six shillings in his pocket and the evening before him. Walking south toward the Bank of Ireland and Trinity College and on into Grafton Street, he arrives at Davy Byrne's (Leopold Bloom's 'moral pub') at 21 Duke Street (ref. d), his nose already sniffing 'the curling fumes of punch'.

At Davy Byrne's he meets his friends, but Higgens and Nosey Flynn lack the necessary funds so the party breaks up. Farrington, Paddy Leonard and O'Halloran leave Davy Byrne's and turn back down Grafton Street, retracing Farrington's steps as they head toward O'Connell Bridge. When they arrive at the Ballast Office on Westmoreland Street (ref. e), Farrington suggests the Scotch House, a Dublin bar and lounge which occupied the corner of Hawkins Street and Burgh Quay (ref. f). The three cross D'Olier Street, walk along beside the Liffey as far as Hawkins Street, and, pushing past the whining match-sellers at the door, enter the bar. There they meet Weathers, an *artiste* out of the Tivoli Theatre located just down Burgh Quay at number 12 and 13 (ref. g). Weathers, another counterpart for Farrington in this story, has apparently slipped out of the theatre during the show for a few drinks and has to return, but he promises to meet them all later in Mulligan's.

When the Scotch House closes, the three head down Hawkins Street and around the corner by the Theatre Royal into Poolbeg Street. Mulligan's bar and lounge (ref. h), then at number 8 Poolbeg Street, was only a few steps down White's Lane from the Tivoli; as such it was a popular gathering place for *artistes* and audience from both that theatre and the Theatre Royal. Here

Farrington loses his reputation as a strong man and, having spent the last of his money, misses his opportunity with the actress from the Tivoli. At the end of the evening, we find him awaiting the Sandymount tram on the corner of O'Connell Bridge, a disappointed and defeated man.

As his journey home begins, he passes the Bank of Ireland for the third time that evening, its imposing and sober facade probably a bitter reminder of his own lack of funds. The tram continues into Nassau Street and along Mount Street Lower and Northumberland Road, carrying him southeast and towards the sea (see Map 12). At Haddington Road it turns due east, setting him down on the corner of Shelbourne Road near his home. As he passes by the stone wall of the Beggar's Bush Infantry Barracks (Map 3.16: ref. i), we are reminded that he has entered the old neighbourhood of Beggarsbush, a district of evil repute during the eighteenth and early nineteenth centuries. The barracks was thought to occupy the site of the original bush where beggars and highwaymen sought temporary shelter before foraging out to ply their trades, and something of this early

association can be seen in Farrington's beggared moral and financial circumstances. The site occupied by the north-east corner of the barracks in Joyce's day (the very corner around which Farrington steers his bulk) was until about 1820 the location of an ancient, ruined structure known as Le Fevre's Folly, and the field surrounding this vaulted and bramble-covered folly also provided refuge and a point of ambush for highwaymen, robbers and smugglers, who ruled the neighbourhood unimpeded after dark by any forces of law and order. Weston St John Joyce tells us that the residents of the neighbouring districts — Ringsend, Irishtown, Ballsbridge, Donnybrook and Sandymount — were forced to provide their own protection and, as a result, seldom ventured outside their homes at night. Farrington's own folly that evening supples a modern counterpart, but his is a folly that has left him in a smouldering rage that seeks rather than avoids the dark side of the street. Entering number 16 Shelbourne Road (Map 3.16: ref. j) by the side-door, he finds the fire is out in his life in more ways than one, and he beats his son out of frustration and anger, providing the final

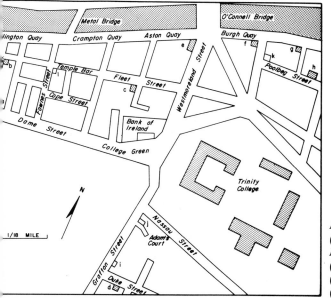

Key to Map 5.26: 'Counterparts': (a) Crosbie and Alleyne; (b) O'Neill's shop; (c) Terry Kelly's pawn office; (d) Davy Byrne's; (e) Ballast Office; (f) Scotch House; (g) Tivoli; (h) Mulligan's of Poolbeg Street; (i) Brown Thomas's ('A Mother'); (j) Empire pub ('Grace'); (k) Theatre Royal ('The Dead'); (l) Liffey Loan Bank ('Grace');

counterpart to the tongue-lashing and bullying he had received from Mr Alleyne at the beginning of the story.

Grace

Joyce wrote to his brother Stanislaus in November 1906 to tell him he had been researching the Vatican Council of 1870 (which declared the infallibility of the Pope) for the story 'Grace'. In that letter he dates the story:

> Grace takes place in 1901 or 2, therefore Kernan at that time, 1870, would have been about twenty-five. He would have been born in 1848 and would have been

only 6 years of age at time of the proclamation of the Immaculate Conception dogma 1854 (*Letters,* II, p. 193).

Stanislaus had already indicated much the same date for the events of the story in an entry in his diary dated 29 September, 1904. He is writing, he says, of an incident which took place about two years earlier:

> Mr Kane [Martin Cunningham of 'Grace'] and Mr Boyd [Jack Power] and Mr Chance [M'Coy] were to attend a retreat in Gardiner Street and Pappie, who would never do anything so vulgar from himself, was persuaded by Mr Kane to attend it too. He did so, and came home very drunk for two nights after each sermon (*Dublin Diary*, p. 77).

The retreat described would have been held soon after John Joyce had moved his family into a residence at 7 St Peter's Terrace off the Phibsborough Road (ref. a), and this is the approximate location for Tom Kernan's house in 'Grace'. Kernan, himself, is based in part on John Joyce (it was he who fell in the bar, injuring his tongue). Born in 1849, he would have been 'about twenty-five' in 1870, as Joyce says in his letter, and, of course, he did attend the retreat for businessmen at the St Francis Xavier Church. For Kernan's personality and occupation, Joyce turned to two neighbours of the family from Richmond Avenue in Fairview. Ned Thornton, Eveline's father, was a commercial traveller for a tea company, probably the London and Newcastle Tea Co. at 61 Thomas Street, which explains the reference in 'Grace' to Kernan's walking to Thomas Street to book an order. The name Thornton does not appear, however, in the list of traders and merchants in the Dublin directories, and there was no tea-company office in Crow Street as the story asserts, though Joyce may have had the tea office located around the corner at 10 Fownes Street in mind. Tom Kernan's name in this story is drawn

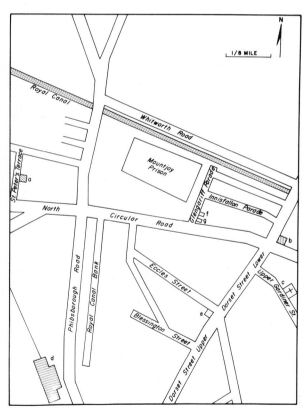

KEY TO MAP 5.27: *"Grace" (a) 7 St Peter's Terrace, Joyce residence (1902); (b) M'Auley's public house; (c) Gardiner Street Church; (d) Midland Railway, Broadstone Station; (e) Larry O'Rourke's public house; (f) 32 Glengariff Parade, Joyce residence (1901); (g) Fogarty's grocery.*

from James M'Kernan, a boot-and-shoe warehouseman whose office was on Talbot Street. This M'Kernan lived next door to the Joyces in Millbourne Lane in Drumcondra and then across the street from them on Richmond Avenue. He must also play a

Mr Power helps Tom Kernan out into Grafton Street and up onto an outsider for the journey to his house on the Glasnevin Road. Adam's Court, site of the Empire Pub, is along the street on the right. Grafton Street (Lawrence Collection NLI).

Left: *View down Adam's Court from the Empire Pub to Grafton St.*
Centre: *St. Peter's Church near Tom Kernan's home contributes to the imagery of 'Grace' in its suggestion of St. Peter's Gate in Dante's* Purgatory.

Right: *7 St Peter's Terrace, the imagined home of Tom Kernan and John Joyce's final house in Dublin.*
Below: *'We can meet in M'Auley's' said Mr M'Coy.' Thomas M'Auley's pub at 39 Dorset St. Close to Gardiner Street Church.*

part in Tom Kernan's personality.

'Grace' begins at the unnamed Empire Buffet on Adam's Court (also unnamed), a small laneway off Grafton Street where Leopold Bloom sees Bob Doran in *Ulysses* (see Map 5.26: ref. j). The Empire served Joyce's purpose well as he set out to organize his story around the three-part division of Dante's *Divine Comedy*. Not only did the Empire have its men's room in the basement, creating an appropriate depth for the fall of man, but its location in the dark, narrow alley in the heart of the city adds to the imagery of hell and contrasts nicely with the journey up and out of the city centre to the Glasnevin Road where Kernan serves his purgatory. Joyce can elicit the 'filth and ooze' and the stifling pressure of a crowded hell (see the sermon episode in *A Portrait*) and at the same time provide a topographical joke for the initiated reader by choosing a bar on *Adam's* Court in order to further the suggestion of man's fall from the grace of Eden. *2/3796*

This unnamed allusion to Adam also helps to explain the reference to the Ballast Office clock in Westmoreland Street which showed half-past nine as the horse-drawn car (an outsider) passed onto O'Connell Bridge on its way to Tom Kernan's house. In Dante, Adam tells us that he was 930 years old when he died and that he spent 4302 years in the first circle of hell before he was rescued by Christ (another 'outsider', called 'the enemy *Power*' in the *Inferno*). It is also worth noting that in the *Purgatorio*, Dante and Virgil pass through St Peter's Gate and begin their climb to the first cornice of Mount Purgatory at nine-thirty on Easter Monday.

If Grafton and Westmoreland Streets serve briefly as the first circles of Dante's hell bordered by the River Acheron (Liffey), then the basement men's room at the Empire Buffet serves as the third circle, where Dante places the gluttonous, those guilty of sins of incontinence, including excessive drinking. In Dante's conception

these sinners lie wallowing in mire unable to communicate with each other (Kernan's injured tongue) and so changed by their torments that Dante cannot recognize those he knew on earth ('The manager of the bar asked everyone who he was and who was with him. No one knew who he was. . . .'). The square stone archway which marks the entrance to Adam's Court also serves to remind us of hell's gate as Dante sees it: high, wide and perpetually unbarred to all those who would enter. In 'Ivy Day in the Committee Room', where some of the same Dantesque imagery is at work, the rain which constantly pelts the gluttonous is falling, but in 'Grace' it is a cold wind that blows off the river to chill the souls of Kernan and Mr Power as they move away from the 'City of Desolation' (Dante also calls hell 'the Empire') towards the suburbs of purgatory.

Joyce has them stop at a house on the Phibsborough Road, and the unstated allusions to Dante continue to pile up. As Map 5.27 shows, John Joyce's house at 7 St Peter's Terrace was just west of this road, while St Peter's Church is located a few steps south of his father's house on the North Circular Road. This is the chapel Mrs Kernan hurries to whenever a wedding is reported, and we are reminded in its name that the entrance to purgatory proper is through St Peter's Gate up the three steps of confession, contrition and satisfaction. Though Kernan only half-heartedly mounts these steps, he does suffer the punishment of the gluttonous in Dante's purgatory — starvation in the sight of plenty — when Mrs Kernan supplies bottles of stout for the visitors but 'nothing for poor little hubby'. The location for Kernan's convalescence is also close to Mountjoy Prison, serving as both a site of punishment and as a refernce to the 'joyful mountain' of purgatory in the *Divine Comedy*. Glasnevin Cemetery, north of Kernan's house and called to our attention when Joyce mentions the Glasnevin

Road, lends another layer to the structure of the story by suggesting a reverse movement on the part of the central character: from hell to the cemetery to the church, perhaps for a second chance at life.

Mr Kernan is convinced to 'wash the pot' with his four friends at the Jesuit church in Gardiner Street (ref. c), but the first premonition that this trip to 'paradise' will not have a lasting redemptive effect comes early in M'Coy's suggestion that they all meet beforehand in M'Auley's, as 'that'll be the most convenient place'. Since it is located just north of the church on Dorset Street (ref. b), it will certainly be convenient, but Joyce does not tell us that M'Auley's is a public house and that Thomas M'Auley will undoubtedly see that they all go well fortified for Father Purdon's sermon. The Church of St Francis Xavier corresponds to Dante's *Paradisio*, but it is a paradise that is debased all along the line. Dante's stopping to drink from the river of Good Remembrance before rising to the first realm of heaven finds its counterpart in the reference to M'Auley's, and much in the short description of the retreat finds similar parallel in Dante. Joyce seems to have the *Paradisio's* first three realms in mind where Dante encounters the souls who were deficient in fortitude, justice and temperance. We are reminded particularly of the third realm (the intemperate) where the discussion centres on the constitution of society and where Dante is lectured on a theme not unlike Father Purdon's, except for the degree of responsibility man must assume. Father Purdon, whose name suggests the infamous Purdon Street in Dublin's brothel district (Map 2.7), is identified by Stanislaus Joyce as Bernard Vaughan, a popular evangelist at the turn of the century. The story ends with Purdon speaking 'to his fellow-men' from the elevated pulpit on the right of the altar with the 'business and professional men' of Dublin arrayed before him like the heavenly host, each according to his rank and degree in the world of Mammon.

In *My Brother's Keeper*, Stanislaus insists on the accuracy of the story and adds:

> Out of sarcastic curiosity I followed them to the church on the last evening of the retreat to listen to the sermon and watch my father fumbling shamefacedly with his lighted candle. The sermon was a man-to-man talk in a chatty tone. I came out into the fresh air before the end. On Saturday they went to confession, and on Sunday morning in a group they approached the alter. On Sunday evening after an outing with his friends, my father came home only moderately drunk with the aforesaid 'Mr Cunningham,' to whom he explained many times over that in confession the priest had told him that 'he wasn't such a bad fellow after all', which authoritative and consoling information caused him both to laugh and to weep (pp. 223-4).

But in spite of its obvious accuracy, of all the stories in *Dubliners*, Joyce took his greatest liberties with the actual places he knew in this story. He places Mr Kernan's house on the Glasnevin Road when in fact his father's house, which served as model, was located to the west of that road, though it seems obvious the name of the terrace and nearby St Peter's Church and school play a role in the symbolic structure of the story. He sets Fogarty's grocery on the same road, but Patrick Fogarty kept his shop at 35 Glengariff Parade (ref. g), two doors away from where the Joyces lived in 1901. Perhaps this uncharacteristic lack of precisely accurate detail can be attributed to the fact that Joyce's father, who was living at the St Peter's address when the story was written, would have been too easily identified had more exact information been used. Just as Joyce chose vacant houses for Bloom and

Paddy Dignam in *Ulysses* where the date can be traced so readily, in *Dubliners* he gives exact locations of private homes only when the occupants he has in mind have moved before the story is written. Considering the trouble he had with publishers and printers over the use of proper names, this is hardly surprising.

The interior of St. Francis Xavier Church where Father Purdon speaks to business men in a business-like way.

Chapter Six

SNOW IS GENERAL

A Mother

Asked by Joyce to comment on the story 'A Mother', Stanislaus replied that he did not like the title (he thought it more appropriate for a painting) but noted, 'the story is done with your usual malicious accuracy' (*Letters*, II, p. 116). He was right. Hardly anywhere do we find a better example of Joyce using the materials of his own experience to give his countrymen a good view of themselves in his 'nicely polished looking-glass'. In August 1904 a series of concerts was given in conjunction with an Irish Industrial Revival Show at the Antient Concert Rooms, 42 Great Brunswick (Pearse) Street (see Map 5.24: ref. L). The concerts began on the afternoon of Monday, 22 August, and continued throughout Horse Show Week with a 'Grand Irish Concert' at 8 o'clock on Saturday evening, 27 August, and two final concerts on the following Monday and Tuesday. Joyce sang at both the first afternoon concert and in the main programme on Saturday evening. This latter concert became the basis for 'A Mother'.

Joyce appears in the story in the role of Mr Bell, the second tenor who shook 'like an aspen'. 'Extremely nervous and extremely jealous of other tenors', Mr Bell had recently been awarded a bronze medal in the Feis Ceoil, a national music competition. Joyce, too, had won the bronze medal in the Feis Ceoil on 16 May, 1904, though unlike Mr Bell, this had been the first and only time Joyce entered the competition (see Ellmann, pp. 156-8). Most of the others appearing at Saturday night's concert, including the headliners J.F. McCormack and J.C. Doyle, have their

counterparts in the story as well:

Concert (August 27, 1904)	'A Mother'
Eileen Reidy, accompanist	Kathleen Kearney
J.F. McCormack	first tenor
J.C. Doyle	baritone
Miss Walker (Marie Nic Shiubhlaigh)	lady who arranged amateur theatricals
Madame Hall	Madam Glynn, the soprano
Miss Agnes Tracey	Miss Healy, the contralto
J.A. Joyce	Mr Bell, second tenor

Also appearing in the story but not named in the advertisements, lists of artists, or reviews of the concert there is Mr Duggen, the bass. Appearing at the Saturday-evening concert but left out of the story are May Reidy, Eileen Reidy's younger sister who gave a cello solo, and Mr George Hillis who played a selection of Irish music on the violin.

In an article entitled 'The Naming of Kathleen Kearney' (*Journal of Modern Literature*, 5 (1976): 532-4) Mary Power has traced the name to an early eighteenth-century song, 'Oh, Did You Not Hear of Kate Kearney', and Joyce could have had this song in mind when he mentioned Mrs Kearney's determination 'to take advantage of her daughter's name' during the height of the Irish Revival. Mr Kearney of the story, however, a bootmaker on Ormond Quay, has his real-life analogue in Mr Joseph Reidy, Eileen's father, and gets his name and occupation from Mr Michael Kearney, a bootmaker at 23 Wexford Street in the city. Joyce rehearsed for the concert at the Reidy home at 15 Mountjoy Street (see Map 6.31) and, according to Eileen Reidy (Ellmann, p. 174), asked for whiskey when her mother offered refreshment; perhaps he was served from the same decanter and silver biscuit-barrel he mentions in the story.

The importance of tracing and examining Joyce's surface naturalism in these stories lies in seeing where he decided to alter reality for the sake of focus or artistic unity. In 'A Mother' he has altered what 'he has seen and heard' in order to remove what might have been an emphasis on his own plight when the accompanist left before he sang, and to place it instead on Mrs Kearney's disillusionment in the face of Irish cultural provincialism. Mr Bell of the story is first on the programme whereas Joyce sang after Eileen Reidy's departure; Joyce gives the factual basis of the story in a letter to his son thirty years later:

Strange coincidence. In my first public concert I too was left in the lurch. The pianist, that is the lady pianist, had gone away right in the middle of the concert. I too sang 'Down by the Sally Gardens' and I received exactly 10 dollars or 2 guineas, like you (*Letters*, III, p. 340).

Without a competent accompanist, Joyce had to alter the programme he had prepared and ended up accompanying himself. Perhaps there was something, however, to the point in the story that the *Freeman* reporter could not remain for the concert (though there is no report in the newspapers of the following days of a talk given by an American priest at the Mansion House) because the review of the concert which appeared in the *Freeman's Journal* on Monday, August 29, seems almost a set-piece and is at odds with Joseph Holloway's first-hand account of the evening. The *Freeman* article gives us the bare details of the concert but does not mention Eileen Reidy's departure, and it reports on the programme Joyce *was* to have sung rather than noting the last-minute change:

Saturday Night's Concert
A concert was given in the large hall of the Antient Concert Rooms on Saturday

The Antient Concert Rooms where Joyce sang in 1904. Once the home of Yeats's A New Irish Literary Theatre, today it is a cinema.

night, and attracted a full house. The programme was a first-rate one. The Exhibition Spring Band played selections of Irish melodies and of operatic music of Irish composers. Mr. J.C. Doyle sang a number of songs in a first-rate style . . . Miss Agnes Treacy [*sic*] sang charmingly a number of Irish airs in Gaelic and English . . . Mr. J.A. Joyce, the possessor of a sweet tenor voice, sang charmingly 'The Salley Gardens', and gave a pathetic rendering of 'The Croppy Boy'. Madame Halle [*sic*] gave a rendering of a number of Irish ballads. Mr. George Hillis played excellently an Irish selection on the violin. Miss May Reidy contributed a violoncello solo. Miss Marie Nic Shiubhlaigh is a lady of considerable histrionic talent, and her selection for recitation gave an opportunity for the display of ·her powers in narrative, the pathetic and the impassioned, all of which she realized fully. She was not so successful in a recitative rendering of one of Mr. Yeats' poems . . . Mr. J.F. M'Cormack was the hero of the evening. It was announced as his last public appearance in Ireland, and the evident feeling of the audience at the parting seemed to unnerve him a good deal. In the interval and after the concert the audience inspected the stalls in the Exhibition.

This is the report of someone who heard only part of the concert, and Joseph Holloway's invaluable diary provides the facts:

The substitute appointed as accompanist in place of Miss Eileen Reidy, who left early in the evening, was so incompetent that one of the vocalists, Mr. James A. Joyce, had to sit down at the piano and accompany himself in the song 'In Her Simplicity', after she had made several unsuccessful attempts to strum out 'The Croppy Boy', the item programmed over the singer's name (Ellmann, p. 174).

Holloway's account also recalls the clamour from the auditorium which Joyce reports in the story. His diary complains that 'the Irish Revivalists are sadly in need of a capable manager' who could see that the programme would begin at the time advertised. This concert, he notes, was no exception: 'the delay was so long that the audience became quite noisy and irritable.'

'A Mother' belongs to the section of *Dubliners* which Joyce devoted to an examination of public life in Dublin. Along with 'Ivy Day in the Committee Room' and 'Grace', Joyce is able to look at politics, religion, and culture as each had become debased in the Dublin he knew. The Antient Concert Rooms had associations which fit this purpose well.

On 8 May, 1899, the Irish Literary Theatre, established two years earlier at Coole, staged its first productions at the Antient Concert Rooms: *The Countess Cathleen* (Yeats) and *The Heather Field* (Edward Martyn). Though the first was condemned by a group of university students (see *Portrait of an Artist:* Joyce refused to sign the petition) and both by the Irish Language Movement, Joyce saw in the productions the beginnings of a break with the parochialism of nineteenth-century Irish literature. He had hoped this would be a start, leading, as the new theatre had promised, to the presentation of the European masters and to providing a continental model for the aspiring Irish artist. He had been particularly pleased with Ibsen's influence on Martyn and wrote his own Ibsenite play, *A Brilliant Career,* after seeing *The Bending of the Bough* by Martyn and George Moore. His disappointment and disillusionment in 1901 when the Irish Literary Theatre staged Douglas Hyde's Gaelic *Casadh an tSugain* and Yeats's *Diarmuid and Grania* led to his pamphlet *The Day of the Rabblement* (1901) and to his assertion that the Irish Literary Theatre, in courting favour with the multitude, had fallen victim to 'its fetishism and deliberate self-deception' and 'by its surrender to the trolls has cut itself adrift from the line of advancement' (*The Critical Writings*, p. 71). These productions were the last of the Irish Literary Theatre and by the time Joyce came to sing at the Antient Concert Rooms the new theatre of Ireland had become the Irish National Dramatic Company, had produced AE's *Deirdre* and Yeats's *Cathleen ni Houlihan* to popular acclaim, and had moved to its new quarters in the old Mechanics Institute and adjoining city

morgue in Abbey and Marlborough Streets.

The Antient Concert Rooms, however, remained in Joyce's mind as the site of the surrender, and the fact that at the time of the concert the Rooms shared the building at 42 Great Brunswick with the Commercial Loan Fund Society, the Socialist Party of Ireland, the Irish Women Franchise League and the Dublin Window Cleaning Company only strengthens Joyce's point about the position culture occupied in Dublin.

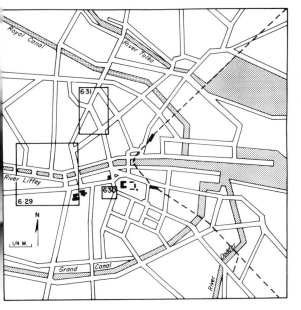

Map 6.28. Locates maps 6.29 ('The Dead'); 6.30 ('Ivy Day'); 6.31 ('The Boarding House').

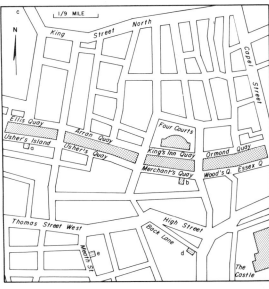

Map 6.29: 'The Dead': (a) The Misses Morkan's, 15 Usher's Island; (b) Adam and Eve's Church; (c) Stoney Batter; (d) Starch Mill in Back Lane; (c) St Catherine's Church ('The Sisters'); (f) Sub-Sheriff's office ('Grace').

The Dead

Usher's Island, cut off from south Dublin by the flow of the Liffey in mediaeval times, had been the site of the famous School of the Friar's Preachers. With the combination of skill and good luck Joyce displayed in finding correspondences, meaningful and otherwise, he is able to set 'The Dead' in another, more modern school at this ancient location. The Misses Morkan's, as it is called in that story, was the home and music school of Mrs Callanan and Mrs Lyons (Aunt Kate and Aunt Julia), listed in *Thom's Dublin Directory* for 1890 as 'The Misses Flynn, teachers of voice and piano-forte'. These women, aunts of Joyce's mother, gave their lessons in the large front room over the cornfactor's office at 15 Usher's Island (ref. a) and were known in the Joyce family for their annual Christmas dinner and dance where John Joyce would carve the goose and deliver the after-dinner speech. Long before that time, the construction of quays which narrowed and straightened the Liffey had brought the island into the south bank, but the historical site, remembered now only in the name of the quay, has a double function in this story. It suggests Gabriel Conroy's final recognition that he is alone in his life, cut off, as an island from the mainland, by a passion in his wife's past which he cannot share (her own thoughts late that night are symbolically restricted to their own island, Nun's Island in Galway City). Secondly, Usher's Island, with its associations historical and ancient, serves as an appropriate location for the counterpoint of topographical forces (western and Gaelic *vs.* eastern and continental) which dominates much of the story.

The 'dark, gaunt house' on Usher's Island encompasses numbers 15 and 16, a three-storey brick building used now in its entirety for the offices of the Dardis and Dunns Seed Company. In 1890 the 'Misses Flynn' shared the premises with M. Smith and Son (also seed merchants) who occupied only part of the ground floor (see Fig. 4). The large, ornate main entrance is on the left of the building, giving onto a hall which at that time ran along beside the seed merchants' quarters. At the end of this short hall, a double-doored archway provides access to the pantry on the right and the banistered staircase rising in its first flight to a broad landing dominated by an arched window. A second flight turns back towards the front of the house to rise the rest of the way to the first-floor hall. Gretta Conroy stands near the top of the first flight late in the story listening to the strains of the 'Lass of Aughrim' while Gabriel watches her from the darkened hall below. In the beginning of the story, however, Aunt Kate and Aunt Julie are stationed at the top of the second flight and thus cannot see down into the hall. Each time they hear the door, they have to call to Lily at the foot of the stairs to learn who has arrived. Those commentators who have seen this as an unnecessary affectation on the old ladies' part did not have a clear understanding of the setting as Joyce must have visualized it.

The second story of the 'Misses Flynn's' was taken up by a front drawing-room (in this story used for dancing) and a back music room (here containing the refreshment tables and serving as the location for the formal supper). A landing and hall at the top of the stairs gave access to both of these rooms (there was no connecting door between them) as well as to the bathroom located over the downstairs hall. For this evening the bathroom had been converted into a ladies' dressing-room. Of the three second-storey windows visible on the front of the house, one belonged to this dressing-room, the other two to the front drawing-room, and when Gabriel retires to the embrasure of a window to think about his after-dinner speech, it is to one of these windows in the drawing-room. Though the snow-capped Wellington Monument in Phoenix Park which comes to his mind is clearly visible from the footpath in front of

Figure 4: The Misses Morkan's, 15 Usher's Island.

Front Elevation

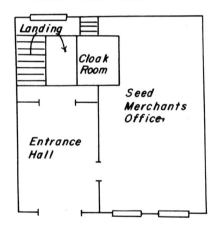

Ground Floor Plan

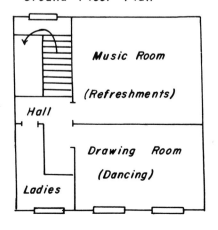

First Floor Plan

15 Usher's Island, it cannot be seen from behind these windows.

Professor Ellmann has provided a detailed examination of the biographical background of 'The Dead' (*James Joyce*, pp. 252-63), identifying Michael Furey of this story with Sonny Bodkin who courted Nora Barnacle in Galway, suffered from tuberculosis, worsened his condition by leaving his sickbed to sing in the rain outside her window as she was preparing to leave for Dublin, and who died of complications soon after she left. Nora had been living with her grandmother on Nun's Island in Galway (as had Gretta Conroy of 'The Dead') and Ellmann notes that she was first attracted to Joyce because he reminded her of Sonny Bodkin. In most other respects, however, Gabriel and Gretta of this story are based more on Joyce's father and mother than on Nora and Joyce himself. As a child, his mother had attended the Misses Flynn's school, not at 15 Usher's Island, as Professor Ellmann says, but at 16 Ellis Quay across the Liffey where the aunts lived during these years (1865-78). By the time John Joyce and Mary (Mae) Murray had married, however, Mrs Lyons, Mrs Callanan and her daughter Mary Jane Callanan had moved to Usher's Island. According to Stanislaus's diary, this latter address served as the location for the annual Christmas party, and it was common for John Joyce and his wife to travel to the city from their home on Northumberland Avenue in Kingstown or later from Bray or Blackrock for the party, and for them to spend the night at the Gresham Hotel on Sackville Street before returning home the next day. It was John Joyce's mother (like Gabriel's) who stood so strongly opposed to his marriage (thinking he had married below himself), and it was Mae Murray's grandfather Flynn who kept the starch mill in Back Lane (ref. d). Of course 'The Dead' is not biography, and Gabriel, with his self-doubts and precarious hold on life, is essentially unlike either Joyce or his father.

Gabriel has gathered the elements of a cosmopolitan modernity around him, elements which do not suffice on this evening against the onslaught of the past. That Joyce places him symbolically suspended on an 'island' near the centre of paralysis, while the forces of the past (here associated with the west of Ireland) bring their pressure to bear, forebodes the final episode of the story.

Throughout 'The Dead' there is a dual alignment of topographical factors underlying the conflict which will emerge in Gabriel Conroy's life. His own predilection is toward the east, the Continent, the cosmopolitan elements of a cosmopolitan Dublin. In his world one wears goloshes and gilt-rim glasses, reviews British poetry, and spends the summer bicycling in France or Belgium. Against this, Miss Ivors stands in direct opposition to Gabriel; she has discovered her Gaelic past and plans a trip far to the west of Ireland for the summer. She draws Gretta's attention to the west (as does the song 'The Lass of Aughrim'), presaging the whole story of her Galway past and the boy who died for love. In the end, Gabriel's feeble attempt towards the

The ground floor hallway leading to the pantry and staircase at 15 Usher's Island.

Gabriel 'was in a dark part of the hall gazing up the staircase. A woman was standing near the top of the first flight in the shadow also . . .'

The Misses Morkan's, 15 Usher's Island. 'The dark gaunt house . . . the upper part of which they had rented from Mr Fulham, the corn-factor on the ground floor.'

Above: *The Gresham Hotel in O'Connell Street where Gabriel and Gretta spend the night in 'The Dead'. (Lawrence Collection, NLI).* Below: *'Across the river, the palace of the Four Courts stood out menacingly against the heavy sky.'*

future crumbles before the ghost of Michael Furey, and he finds himself caught up in the dead past, resigned to begin his own 'journey westward'. Long before the concluding episode, however, the topographical details have been arranged to push Gabriel towards the moment when he will surrender to the west, recognizing the elements of his urbanity as self-delusion.

Gabriel has come to 15 Usher's Island from Monkstown, lying to the south-east and near the sea. Significantly, he announces at the outset that he does not intend to return that night, and, of course, we will see that psychologically he will never return to the east again. Instead, he is to spend the night at the Gresham Hotel (see Map 7.34: ref. e), a short journey from Usher's Island taking him to the very centre of Dublin and to a stasis where he is left gazing directly west from the window of his room. In keeping with this, his own attention tends more and more to the west as the evening progresses. As he stands in the embrasure of the drawing-room window, he imagines the Wellington Monument lying due west of 15 Usher's Island, and though he may not realize it, is gazing along the quay once known as Lord Galway's Walk before it was changed to Victoria Quay to honour the queen's

visit. Just before beginning his after-dinner speech he again pictures the snow falling in the Phoenix Park, this time 'over the white field of Fifteen Acres' (see Map 28), a site even farther west than the monument. The old aunts, associated in Gabriel's toast with the traditional virtues of Ireland (and silently to himself with the tiresome stupidity of old age), also play a part in this movement to stasis. We are told immediately that they have come to their 'island' from Stoney Batter, and since the real aunts had moved instead from Ellis Quay, we can assume Joyce has gone out of his way to include this reference. Stoney Batter, literally the 'road of stones', was once part of the ancient thoroughfare from Tara (the seat of Ireland's kings) to Wicklow, crossing the Liffey at the Ford of Hurdles (*Atha Cliath*). As such, it serves as both another reminder of the forces of the past and also as a suggestion that these women have left the road which might lead to escape from Ireland. Gabriel will sit alone in his life on the 'island' of the Gresham Hotel, thinking his way from east to west, from Sackville Street to the Bog of Allen in the central plains to the Shannon River flowing into the Atlantic, and we will know that he, too, has abandoned the road to escape.

Left: *The shooting-lodge in Killikee, Co. Dublin where the Hell-Fire Club worshipped the devil (Lawrence Collection, NLI).*

Right: *Wicklow Street, the site of the committee room (number 15) where Parnell is abandoned once again.*

Below: *'He is dead. Our Uncrowned King is dead.' The lying-in-state of Charles Stewart Parnell, Dublin City Hall, October 1891. (Lawrence Collection, NLI).*

Ivy Day in the Committee Room

In January 1903 Stanislaus Joyce served with his father on an election committee, and his account of the incident, sent to his brother in Paris, gave Joyce the central idea for his favourite story, 'Ivy Day in the Committee Room'. When Stanislaus read the story later in manuscript, he called it 'accurate, just, and satisfactory' (*Letters*, II, p. 115), though he noted in the same letter that it would be 'highly improbable' (p. 114) for a municipal election to take place in October. Joyce persisted in that detail, however, because he wanted to set the story on 6 October, 1902, the anniversary of Charles Stewart Parnell's death and a few months prior to King Edward VII's visit to Ireland (the following July). To further emphasize the ghost of 'the un-crowned king of Ireland' hovering in the background, Joyce places the election committee on Wicklow Street, reminding us that Parnell's ancestral estate was located in that county and that Parnell was a member for Wicklow as well as leader of the Irish Parliamentary Party. But Joyce goes even another step, for those who know Wicklow Street, in establishing this correspondence. The only place on this street for the story to have taken place is in one of the dark, upper rooms at the back of the Central Chambers then at number 15 Wicklow (ref. a). This establishes a connection with Parnell's parliamentary defeat in Committee Room 15 at Westminster and suggests that, like the sinners of Dante's hell, these modern remnants of Parnell's party must come together once again to reenact the 'crime' of abandoning their leader.

Across the street from the Central Chambers Joyce had two pubs to choose from for O'Farrell's where the boy borrows the corkscrew, one at 37 Wicklow and the other at 39. Joyce probably had Thomas O'Neill's shop (ref. c) at number 37 in mind, and he probably borrowed the name from Patrick Farrell's pub at 21 Grafton Street (ref. b), around the corner from the committee room. He had already used another O'Neill's in 'Counterparts' and Farrell's was in his mind because it serves as the location of the other pub in the story, the Black Eagle. It was placed right for the details of the story, and it is the kind of fashionable bar Dick Tierney would have owned. The Black Eagle also supports the underlying connection with Parnell, recalling Joyce's use of the fallen eagle as symbol for Parnell whose name had been blackened by the 'coward hounds' of Church and State. On another level, the name of this pub supports the second structural element of the story which casts the committee room on Wicklow Street as a kind of hell where Old Jack, the caretaker, fans the cinders which reveal his hairy devil's face.

Whenever Joyce alters the details of the Dublin he knew by setting a story in a location other than the one at which it really took place, or by changing the name

Map 6.30: 'Ivy Day in the Committee Room': (a) Committee Room on Wicklow Street; (b) Black Eagle pub; (c) O'Farrell's; (d) Wicklow Hotel (A Portrait); (e) Barnardo's (A Portrait).

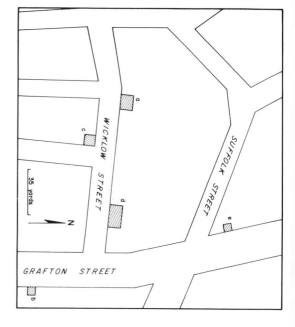

of a restaurant or public house, we should take special note for he does it so seldom. When he does, he is usually trying to draw our attention to part of the underlying structure. In this case the allusion is to the 'Hellfire Club' founded by Old Jack St Leger in 1735. He and his infamous band of devil-worshippers met in a pub called the Eagle Tavern located on nearby Cork Hill in Dublin (see Map 5.25), and legend has it that they set a shooting-lodge in the foothills of the Dublin mountains afire during one gathering, the better to experience the flames of hell. In Joyce's more modern analogue, Tricky Dicky Tierney has not supplied enough coal for any such conflagration, but he sends along the 'demon drink' to sound its feeble three-gun salute to the dead Chief. Joyce suffuses the room at 15 Wicklow with the 'darkness-visible' of Milton's hell (echoed later at the Belvedere retreat in *A Portrait*) and fills his story with references to the devil. 'Talk of the devil', Henchy says as Crofton enters, and Fr Keon is a fallen priest (angel) while Tricky Dicky is the 'mean little shoe-boy of hell'. Henchy himself passes judgement on Lyons ('Blast your soul') and rubs his hands together as if like the devil, he could produce sparks from his finger tips. But there are no sparks in his degenerate hell of modern Dublin politics, and Parnell has been abandoned again, his party in the hands of opportunists such as Tierney and his memory reduced to an occasion for sentimentality in Joe Hyne's doggerel verse.

The Boarding House

In this story Bob Doran sits, trapped and immobile, near the very centre of the 'centre of paralysis' on Hardwicke Street just west of Belvedere College. Though Joyce conceived this story in Trieste 'while the sweat streamed down [his] face' (*Letters*, II, p. 98), drawing it from comments related to him by a fellow English teacher in the Berlitz school about his landlady and her daughter, he sets the story at the 'Waverley' at number 4 Hardwicke Street (ref. a), the only boarding house on that street in Joyce's day.

The clearest picture of Hardwicke Street at the turn of the century comes from Somerville and Ross (*The Real Charlotte*, 1894), reprinted in Maurice Craig's study of Dublin architecture:

> An August Sunday afternoon in the north side of Dublin. Epitome of all that is hot, arid, and empty. Tall brick houses, browbeating each other in gloomy respectability across the white streets . . . Stifling squares . . . Few towns are duller out of season than Dublin, but the dullness of its north side neither waxes nor wanes . . . the emptiness of the streets, the unvarying dirt of the window panes, and the almost forgotten ugliness of the window curtains (pp. 296-7).

Joyce sets his story on another summer Sunday and, though a morning breeze wafts the lace curtains of the boarding house gently towards the street and Bob Doran would like to rise on that breeze and 'ascend through the roof and fly away to another country', Joyce has gathered the paralyzing forces of Dublin around him, and Mrs Mooney has good reason to feel 'sure she would win'. At one end of Hardwicke Street, St George's Church (ref. b) sends out constant peals to its Protestant worshippers and a constant reminder to Doran of his 'religious duty' and of the confession which the priest had drawn out of him the night before. Bracketing the other end of the street is the Catholic wine-merchant's office, W. and A. Gilby, at 58 Dorset Street (ref. c) where he has worked for thirteen years and where he imagines the rasping voice of old Mr Leonard should he attempt an escape. Hardwicke Street itself carries the stern reminder of moral duty in that it had been the first home of the Jesuit Order after the restoration of that society in Ireland and the location of the first Dublin College of St Francis Xavier, the predecessor of Belvedere on Denmark Street.

With Mrs Mooney 'sharpening her cleaver' in the parlour, Polly's brother with his 'thick bulldog face' glaring from the banister, and Polly sobbing softly in his bedroom, the forces of moral Dublin have brought all their pressure to bear. Bob Doran can find no way out, and later in *Ulysses* when Leopold Bloom catches sight of him 'sloping' into the Empire Pub 'on his annual bend', we are not and should not be surprised.

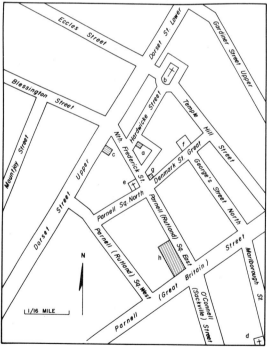

Map 6.31: 'The Boarding House': (a) Mrs Mooney's boarding house; (b) St George's Church; (c) Catholic Wine Merchant's Office; (d) Pro-Cathedral in Marlborough Street; (e) Findlater's Church (A Portrait); (f) Belvedere College (A Portrait); (g) Cigar shop (A Portrait); (h) Rotunda Concert Rooms ('A Painful Case').

The Waverley Boarding House on the corner at number 4 Hardwicke Street.

Chapter Seven

WHERE THE CORKSCREW WAS

Clay

The movement in 'Clay' is easy to trace: as Maria herself says, 'From Ballsbridge to the Pillar, twenty minutes; from the Pillar to Drumcondra, twenty minutes; and twenty minutes to buy the things' (see Map 7.32). Its significance lies in the way it reinforces both the religious and supernatural elements of the story, when Maria as the Virgin Mary and Maria as Halloween witch travels from the Protestant Dublin-by-Lamplight Laundry to the 'Holy Land' of Drumcondra.

Marvin Magalaner and Richard Kain (*Joyce: the Man, the Work, the Reputation,* pp. 84-91) have seen, along with many others now, that Maria's character combines elements of both the peace-maker and the trouble-maker and that it is not inconsequential that 'Clay' (originally titled 'Hallow Eve') takes place on 31 October, the night when spirits walk abroad and the Eve of All Saints' Day when the blessed of the world, those canonized and those unknown, are honoured. What has not been noted before, however, is the way in which the topography plays a role in what Florence Walzl ('"Clay": An Explication') calls the 'conflicting elements in Maria' which 'suggests saint and witch', and how more is 'out of joint' on this evening than may at first seem apparent.

The Dublin-by-Lamplight Institution at 35 Ballsbridge Terrace (Map 7.33) is described in *Thom's Directory* as a 'valuable institution . . . supported by voluntary contributions and by the inmates own exertions'. It was a charitable institute with a working laundry attached, organized under the auspices of the Protestant Church of Ireland and catering for home-less women who otherwise, the name suggests, might be plying their trade beneath the street-lamps of Dublin. The laundry's biblical motto, 'That they may recover themselves out of the snare of the devil, who are taken captive by him at his will' (2 Tim., ii, 26), was not lost on Joyce who had this to say about the laundry's name in a letter to his brother:

> You ask me to explain . . . the meaning of *Dublin by Lamplight* Laundry? That is the name of the laundry at Ballsbridge, of which the story treats. It is run by a society of Protestant spinsters, widows, and childless women — I expect — as a Magdalen's home. The phrase *Dublin by Lamplight* means that Dublin by lamplight is a wicked place full of wicked and lost women whom a kindly committee gathers together for the good work of washing my dirty shirts (*Letters,* II, p. 192).

Both the motto and Joyce's phrase, 'wicked and lost women', suggest that the 'valuable institution' in Ballsbridge may indeed be a den of witches, and Maria's physical description coupled with the remark in the first sentence that this evening, 31 October, was 'her evening out' strengthens the conceit.

Maria, a relative of Joyce's mother (see *Letters,* II, p. 147), worked in the kitchen of the institute, and in the story she keeps the 'cauldrons' well-polished and, as if by magic, slices the barmbracks so neatly they appear uncut. In her other role as Mary the saint, she is cast as a 'veritable peace-maker' at the laundry and always sent for when the other women quarrel.

Top: *Ballsbridge. Maria takes a tram from the bridge to Nelson's Pillar in the city centre.*
Left: *'She went into Downe's cake-shop.' Kylemore Cakes now occupies the premises on North Earl Street.*

Bottom: *'Maria understood that it was wrong that time . . . this time she got the prayer-book.' — St Alphonsus's Convent, Drumcondra.*

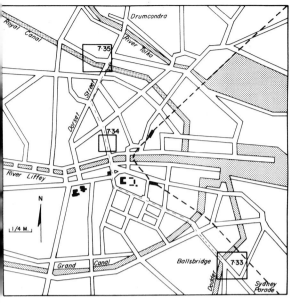

Map 7.32. 'Clay' (Insets identify maps 7.33 (Ballsbridge); 7.34 (City Centre); 7.35 (Drumcondra).

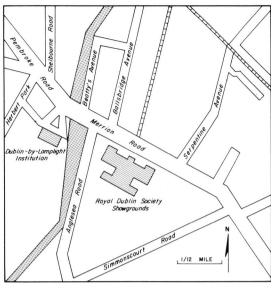

Map 7.33. 'Clay': Ballsbridge.

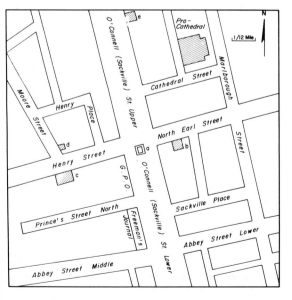

Map 7.34 'Clay': City centre (a) The Pillar; (b) Downe's cake shop; (c) Mullen's cake shop, Henry Street; (d) Butler's of Moore Street ('Grace'); (e) Gresham Hotel ('The Dead').

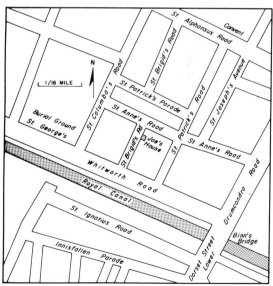

Map 7.35. 'Clay': Drumcondra.

But if 'Everyone was so fond of Maria' at the institute where she spread nothing but peace and happiness, her evening visit to Joe's house has very much the opposite effect. Losing the plum cake on the way, she upsets the children by suggesting they might have taken it and goes on to generally disrupt the evening through a series of well-intentioned blunders. This contrast between Maria as competent witch and saint at the laundry and Maria at Joe's where she fails at both roles is central to the story, and Joyce is careful to select widely divergent locations to emphasize and lend irony to the contrast.

For Maria, the institute in Ballsbridge should represent an alien environment if we can believe the picture she gives us of herself. There she is detached from her 'family and children', constantly reminded by the 'tracts' on the wall of a religion not hers, and even separated from her fellow inmates by their broader coarseness. If we take Joyce's reference to a Magdalen's home to suggest that the other biblical Mary is also carried in Maria's name, we have to admit that, unlike what we see in the others, she at least is neither a reformed nor a potential prostitute. Beyond this, the whole village of Ballsbridge seems alien to Maria's character. Dominated by the Royal Dublin Society Agricultural Building and Showgrounds, the neighbourhood was a Protestant-ascendancy enclave and a popular venue for visitors from England, particularly during the Society's flower shows and during Horse-Show Week every August. Yet this is the place where Maria is most successful, where her 'magic' works best, where her maternal instincts are readily received even if they do only extend to settling quarrels and raising impotent ferns and wax plants. At Joe's house, on the other hand, she should feel right at home and be the most effective. Not only does it represent the bosom of her family, remembering that she was Joe's 'proper mother', but, as a look at Map 7.35 will show, she is symbolically immersed there in her religion. Appropriate both to Maria's piety and to All Saints' Day Eve, she is surrounded by no fewer than nine saints represented in the street names of Joe's neighbourhood. Saints Columba, Alphonsus, Patrick, Anne, Clement, Ignatius, George, Brendan and Joseph are

'Everybody said: O, here's Maria! when she came to Joe's house' on St Brigid's Road Lower, Drumcondra.

all there to welcome her on this night, and nowhere else in Dublin could Joyce have found a denser concentration of saints' names than he did here in Lower Drumcondra.

For Joe's house itself Joyce uses the home of his Uncle John Murray at 55 St Brigid's Road Lower. It is clear from the details of the story that Maria is heading towards that street when she leaves the tram at Binn's Bridge, and Joyce points clearly to the same destination when he alludes to his uncle (he called him the Marquis of Lorne) in reference to this story:

> I have also added in the story, *The Clay,* the name of Maria's laundry, the *Dublin by Lamplight Laundry:* it is such a gentle way of putting it. I expect there will be no holding the Marquis of Lorne [John Murray] whenever he sees my book. (*Letters,* II, p. 186, and see p. 192).

Professor Ellmann also points out the use of John Murray in this story, noting that Joe's brother, Alphy, is based on John's brother, William Murray, who figures in 'Counterparts'.

Joe's neighbourhood and its topographical detail served Joyce well for this story and may have even suggested some of the story's underlying structure. Not only does Maria find herself on a street bearing the name of the female patron saint of Ireland, but two conspicuous features of the neighbourhood parallel the game of the three dishes in which Maria first selects clay from the garden (death) and then a prayer book (life in a convent). As those familiar with Lower Drumcondra knew, Maria plays out this prophetic game at an appropriate location. Just west of St Brigid's Road, between St Clement's Road and the Drumcondra Hospital, St George's Burial Ground lies awaiting her, while just north of Joe's house, the Convent of the Redemtoristine Nuns founded by St Alphonsus dominates the street bearing that saint's name. Both are so close to John Murray's house that

they must have inescapably been in Joyce's thoughts as he constructed this story.

Dillon Cosgrave (*North Dublin,* pp. 64-5) tells us that the whole district of Drumcondra contained so many religious institutions that it had acquired the name of the 'Holy Land'. Of particular interest to this story, the Missionary College of All Hallows reminds us that the townland of Drumcondra once belonged to the ancient Priory of All Hallows, then situated where Trinity College now stands. The Sacred Heart Home (now Holy Cross College) was just across Drumcondra Road from St Alphonsus's Convent and had served in turn as the early location of this convent and then as the site of St Patrick's Training College before the latter moved north into Drumcondra proper. Yet, in spite of all this spiritual presence (or perhaps because of it), it is at Joe's house that Maria, in the topsy-turvy logic of Hallow's Eve, is least effective. Maybe Joyce is also reminding us that the townland of Puckstown lay close enough to Drumcondra for that ancient and mischievous Irish spirit to exercise his impish control on this evening when plum cakes and nutcrackers and corkscrews seem to disappear without reason.

More likely, however, Joyce wants us to focus on the pathetic incompetence Maria carries about and spreads around her and to conclude that, like Eveline's self-deception about a life with Frank in Buenos Ayres (see Hugh Kenner, *The Pound Era,* pp. 34-9), Maria has created her own fictional story in which to live. In her fiction she is clever and competent, the peacemaker, the 'proper mother'. But all she tells us about herself is incompatible with what we see at the cake shop, on the tram, and at Joe's house. That the whole setting in Lower Drumcondra would seem to be so harmonious to Maria's success only emphasizes her failure there and further calls her reported success at the laundry into question. Maria's character does indeed carry elements of both the Virgin Mary and

Kingston Harbour. 'They got into a rowboat at the ship and made out for the American's yacht. There was to be supper, music and cards.' (Lawrence Collection, NLI)

bedevilling, unwanted 'witch', but the first
is part of her own fictional self-deception,
the second the reality of her life.

As for the middle part of her journey
(Map 7.34), we are tempted to see her
movements east and west of Nelson's Pillar
as further suggestion of the two Marys
carried in her name. Her walk to Downes's
cake shop takes her into North Earl Street,
already established in 'Two Gallants' (and
well-known in Joyce's Day) as the main
entrance to Dublin's notorious prostitute
district, while her movement west to Annie
Mullen's confectionery at 37 Henry Street
or to Bewley's further along the same street
takes her towards the old and extensive
demense of St Mary's Abbey. She describes
a cross at this point of her journey, and
Joyce was so fond of this kind of symbolic
representation that it would be presump-
tuous to say he did not intend it.

'The street was busy with unusual traffic, loud with the horns of motorists and the gongs of impatient tram drivers'.
A motorist on Grafton Street. (The original glass negative is defective) (Lawrence Collection, NLI)

After the Race

At the beginning of April 1903 Joyce interviewed the French race car driver, Henri Fournier, at his automobile salesroom in Paris. Fournier, described by Joyce in that interview as a 'slim, active-looking young man', was favourite for the French team in the James Gordon Bennett cup race to be held in Ireland the following July. 'Will you remain any time in Ireland?', Joyce asked. 'After the race?', Fournier replied, 'I am afraid not. I should like to, but I don't think I can'. But Joyce, who was in Ireland at the time though he did not attend the race, turned his imagination to the hours following the race and focused his attention not on the sophisticated Fournier (Charles Ségouin) but on a young Dubliner, Jimmy Doyle, in a story where the provincial Irish character is contrasted with the continental. Joyce's own adopted 'voice' in the interview (see *Critical Writings*, pp. 106-8) is not unlike Doyle's feeling of awe as he comes 'scudding in towards Dublin' in the back seat of Ségouin's car.

In order to follow the route Jimmy Doyle and his friends cover at the end of the race we can begin at Rathcoole to the south-west of Dublin and travel along the Naas Road and Tyrconnell Road, crossing Golden Bridge at Inchicore. Emmet Road, Old Kilmainham, and Mount Brown will bring us into James Street, and from there we follow Thomas, High and Lord Edward Streets past the Castle and into Dame Street. Ségouin's car stops in front of the Bank of Ireland at College Green to let Doyle and Villona out and then continues around into Grafton Street heading for Stephen's Green and the Shelbourne Hotel where Ségouin is staying.

The Shelbourne, then as today an upper-class, tourist establishment, is opposed in this story to the north side of Dublin where Jimmy Doyle lives. This division between the pleasant residential areas south of the Liffey and the more depressed north city still exists today. It is not without meaning

in *A Portrait*, when Stephen's move from the southern suburb of Blackrock to Fitzgibbon Street on the north side coincides with his father's dwindling assets and with his own chaotic adolescence. Having experienced his revelation in that novel, Stephen moves towards the southern neighbourhoods as he takes greater control of himself and begins to dominate his surroundings. Of course Jimmy Doyle is not poor as Stephen is and like Gallaher of 'A Little Cloud' he has been to England, but his Irish provincialism is still his most obvious characteristic and Joyce is right to separate him physically from the Frenchman, the Canadian and the Englishman who have, for the evening at least, made the south side their domain. Doyle and Villona (who *is* poor) both experience 'a curious feeling of disappointment' as they part from Ségouin and Rivière and from the relative sophistication of southern Dublin. It is not long, however, before they are all back together in the Shelbourne for dinner, and Jimmy's imagination is once again set afire.

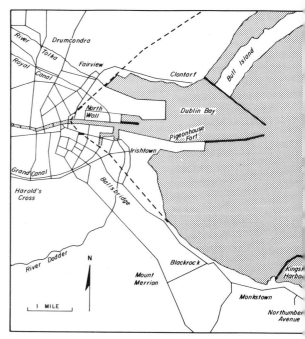

Map. 7.36. 'After the Race'.

As the story progresses, Joyce presents the elements of the setting as if Jimmy Doyle were still 'careering' along in the race car. Yet those elements to which he calls our attention are also representative of Doyle's continental aspirations. The Bank of Ireland, once the seat of Ireland's parliament before its representatives voted to eliminate themselves in the Act of Union; Grafton Street, the Shelbourne and Stephen's Green, all associated with the rich and sophisticated in Dublin; the train south-east from Westland Row to Kingstown where the name of the harbour represents England's firm foothold in Ireland as well as a point of escape to the Continent — these all flash by in the story as Jimmy loses track of the time as well as the cards. As Joyce says early in the story, 'Rapid motion through space elates one; so does notoriety; so does the possession of money.' By the end, however, Jimmy Doyle has come to a dead stop, anchored on the American's yacht in Kingstown Harbour. When Villona stands in the grey light of dawn to announce 'Daybreak, gentlemen!', Doyle has begun to recognize his folly, and though the movement in the story has been from west to east with a constant continental longing, his 'escape' has been as fleeting and non-productive as anywhere in *Dubliners*.

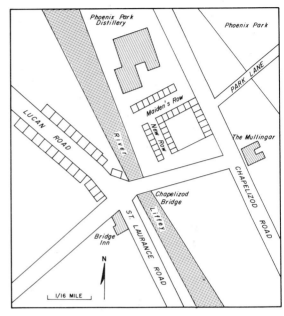

Map 7.38. Chapelizod, 1900.

Map 7.37. 'A Painful Case': (a) Cake shop at Parkgate; (b) Disused distillery; (c) Public house in Chapelizod.

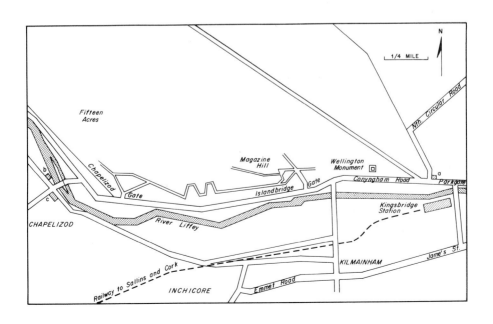

A Painful Case

In *My Brother's Keeper,* Stanislaus Joyce says that while the family lived on Millbourne Lane in Drumcondra in 1894 (see Map 3.13), he had a fight with a boy called 'Pisser' Duffy and that his brother later borrowed the name for the main character of 'A Painful Case'. We find this Duffy in the valuation lists for the Electoral Division of Drumcondra, 1890, located at number 1 Clonturk Avenue, just across the Drumcondra Road and opposite Millbourne Lane. It seems equally likely, however, that Joyce had a Mr James Duffy, a wholesale bookseller at 15-17 Wellington Quay, in mind when he chose the name for this character. He could have hardly missed the large sign over this shop advertising James Duffy and Company as a 'depot for religious goods and Catholic Art repository' as he browsed in the bookshops on the quays, and this Duffy's profession might have helped to suggest the copy of the *Maynooth Catechism* which stood at one end of the character's bookcase in opposition to the complete Wordsworth which stood at the other. Certainly many in Dublin would have known that an edition of this catechism was printed by James Duffy and Company. The character's personality, however, is based in part on Stanislaus himself, and it was he met a married woman at a concert at the Rotunda, giving Joyce the starting-point for his story. Professor Ellmann tells us that the aphorisms, 'Every bond is a bond to sorrow' and 'Love between man and man is impossible because there must not be sexual intercourse and friendship between man and woman is impossible because there must be sexual intercourse', are taken from an early diary Stanislaus kept, a diary Joyce labelled 'Bile Beans' when he read it (*Ellmann*, p. 138).

The central topographical metaphor at work in this story is the suburb of Chapelizod as it relates to the romance of Tristram and Iseult (Izod). The passion of that ancient love story has degenerated in modern Dublin to the prissy behaviour of James Duffy. Every day he follows the set routine (Map 3.16) to work at the private bank in Baggot Street (Joyce uses the Royal Bank of Ireland at number 54 Lower Baggot Street), to the same tasteless lunch two doors away at Dan Burke's pub, to his evening meal always in the same eating house in George's Street. James Duffy is not about to allow a relationship with another individual to upset this life even if he does live at the site where Iseult gave up everything for love. At the end, however, he is drawn to Magazine Hill in Phoenix Park, the legendary location of Iseult's Well where she pledged herself to Tristram. From this height he can see the lovers entwined in the shadow of the wall of the park and can look beyond to the Liffey relentlessly flowing towards Dublin and the trains from Kingsbridge (Heuston) Station relentlessly winding their way to the west. His own life will take on this same relentless quality. "Outcast from life's feast', he will reappear in *Ulysses* as the man in the mackintosh at the Glasnevin Cemetery, visiting again and again, we assume, Mrs Sinico's grave.

James Duffy lived in Chapelizod 'because he found all the other suburbs of Dublin mean, modern and pretentious'. The village was a picturesque and popular residence in Joyce's day, though Duffy's view in this story seems dominated by the then empty Phoenix Park Distillery located just across the River Liffey from his rented rooms. Joyce places him on the east side of the Lucan Road (ref. b) only a few steps north of the Bridge Inn (ref. c), the pub he visits after reading of Mrs Sinico's death. Across the bridge there was another pub, the Mullingar House, which figures prominently as Earwicker's pub in *Finnegans Wake*. At the time of the story, Chapelizod was best known as the setting for Sheridan Le Fanu's gothic novel, *The House by the Churchyard*, and that house still stood next to the Protestant parish church just to the south

Top: *'One evening he found himself sitting beside two ladies in the Rotunda.'*
Bottom: *The Magazine Fort on Thomas's Hill in the Phoenix Park.*
Overleaf: *The disused distillery on the banks of the Liffey at Chapelizod.*

of the bridge. But the village had other, older claims on which to base its air of old-world respectability. A house and extensive lands located on the banks of the Liffey had been acquired by Charles II in the seventeenth century, and when the viceroy's summer residence on Thomas's Hill in Phoenix Park was demolished to make way for the Magazine Fort in 1734, the Irish viceroys moved into that house in Chapelizod, known as the King's House since William III had previously resided there for a few days. It is ironic, but perhaps not unintentional, that James Duffy begins this story on the site of one royal residence and ends at another and that both had been superceded long before by more modern structures.

The Manor House of the Phoenix Park which the Magazine Fort came to replace may in its name and location suggest Duffy's hope that his own spirit might rise from despair if even only to its former complacency, but by having him end his walk at the Magazine Fort, Joyce makes it clear that it is too late for any such rebirth. Most of Dublin would have immediately associated the Fort here with Dean Swift's satiric epigram:

> Behold a proof of Irish sense,
>   Here Irish wit is seen,
> When nothing's left that's worth defence,
>   We build a magazine.

Certainly this applies as well to James Duffy's well-ordered and organized life and how ineffectual a defence it will be now that he has recognized his own loneliness. In antithesis to Iseult, however, who recognized her own defencelessness at this same location, it has been Duffy's refusal to give up anything that has left him nothing.

As for Mrs Sinico of Leoville, Sydney Parade, she seems to be purely an invention of Joyce's imagination. The name is borrowed from Giuseppi Sinico, under whom Joyce studied voice in Trieste (Ellmann, p. 162), but as for the remainder of the story's details, there was no Sinico, of course, on Sydney Parade Avenue in

Dublin (nor for that matter anywhere else in Dublin). Leoville as a house-name Joyce took from the home at 23 Carysfort Avenue in Blackrock where his family lived in 1892. The accident at Sydney Parade Station (see Map 7.32) never occurred according to the officials at that station, and the newspaper article appears also to be totally fictitious as far as an accident at any other station in Dublin is concerned. Joyce suggested as much when he wrote to his brother to ask if a victim at Sydney Parade would be taken to the City of Dublin Hospital (see Map 3.16: ref. n). Stanislaus replied that 'the City Ambulance would be called out to Sydney Parade at the time the story is supposed to have occurred . . . but in all probability the body would have been sent in on the tram' (*Letters,* II, p. 115). Joyce kept the ambulance in the story, however, but it seems that his selection of Sydney Parade for Mrs Sinico's home was dictated less by an interest in the City of Dublin Hospital than by his wish to contrast her residence with Duffy's Chapelizod lying in the west and in its past. As a result, Duffy turns away from the east and the sea, the future and companionship all at the same time when he turns from Mrs Sinico's gesture of love. It turns out to be a very painful case for all involved.

'*When Mr Duffy came to the public-house at Chapelizod Bridge he went in and ordered a hot punch.' Bridge Inn on the St. Laurence Road.*

Principal Joyce Residences

47 Northumberland Avenue, Kingstown
41 Brighton Square, Rathgar (1882)
23 Castlewood Avenue, Rathmines (1884)
1 Martello Terrace, Bray (1887) Map 1
23 Carysfort Avenue, Blackrock (1892) Map 3
14 Fitzgibbon Street (1893) Map 5
2 Millbourne Villas (1894) Map 8
17 North Richmond Street (1895) Map 4
29 Windsor Avenue, Fairview (1898) Map 10
13 Richmond Avenue, Fairview (1899) Map 10
8 Royal (Inverness) Terrace, Fairview (1900) Map 10
32 Glengariff Parade (1901) Map 8
7 St Peter's Terrace, Cabra (1902)
60 Shelbourne Road (1904) Map 12

The Kingstown residence belonged to John and May Joyce before James was born.

The family occupied other addresses for very short periods during Joyce's years in Dublin. Between the Blackrock address and the house in Fitzgibbon Street, the family stayed in rented rooms at 29 Hardwicke Street for about a month, and before finding a house on Windsor Avenue in Fairview, they stayed with the Hughes family at 19 Richmond Avenue for a few weeks. Joyce left his father's house at the end of 1902 and spent four months in Paris. After his return, he moved in and out of a rented room at 60 Shelbourne Road, stayed six nights with St John Gogarty in the Martello Tower at Sandycove, and lived for a while with James Cousins in Ballsbridge, and with his uncle, William Murray, on the Strand Road in Sandymount. He may also have stayed a few nights in a rented room at 35 Strand Road, Sandymount.

Sydney Parade Station: 'The company had always taken every precaution to prevent people crossing the lines except by the bridges.'

GLOSSARY AND INDEX OF PLACE-NAMES in *A PORTRAIT OF THE ARTIST AS A YOUNG MAN* and *DUBLINERS*

The page numbers which follow each item refer to the standard editions of each book: *A Portrait of the Artist as a Young Man* (Viking Press, 1964) and *Dubliners* (Viking Press, 1968). Other editions may vary by a page or two. Each item is given as it appears in Joyce's text; the definitions, whenever possible, are as they appear in books describing turn-of-the-century Dublin. Map references are to the maps in this book where the items will be most readily found (5.24 refers to Chapter 5, Map No. 24).

THE ACADEMY ("The Dead": 160)
Royal Academy of Music, 36 Westland Row. Map 5.24.

ADAM AND EVE'S ("The Dead": 160)
Franciscan Chapel of Adam and Eve, Merchant's Quay. Map 6.29.

ADELPHI HOTEL (*PORTRAIT*: 237)
20-21 Anne Street South. Map 3.16.

ALLEGHANIES (*PORTRAIT*: 35)
Mountain range in the eastern United States known particularly as an area settled by Scots and Irish immigrants in the eighteenth and nineteenth centuries. Mrs 'Dante' Hearn Conway, Joyce's governess, was a novice in a convent there before her brother, who made his fortune trading with African natives, died and left her £30,000 (Ellmann, p. 24).

ALLEY BEHIND THE NATIONAL UNIVERSITY (*PORTRAIT*: 200)
This alley is located between the Newman university chapel and the principal university building at 86 St Stephen's Green South. Map 3.16.

ANTIENT CONCERT ROOMS ("A Mother": 126, "The Dead": 160)
The Concert Rooms included a large hall on the ground floor and a smaller hall on the first floor at 42 Great Brunswick (Pearse) Street. John Joyce sang there in 1875, and his son, James, followed him on 27 August, 1904, successfully overcoming the difficulty caused when the accompanist, Miss Eileen Reidy, left during the interval. Map 5.24.

ARABY BAZAAR ("Araby": 27)
The Araby bazaar was held from 14 to 19 May, 1894, at the Royal Dublin Society Showgrounds in Ballsbridge. Map 7.33.

ARKLOW (*PORTRAIT*: 36)
A town in south-eastern Co. Wicklow about thirty-eight miles south of Dublin. Avondale, Parnell's ancestral home, is located between Rathdrum and the Vale of Avoca, Co. Wicklow. Map 1.1.

ATHY (*PORTRAIT*: 25)
A town in Kildare about twenty-five miles south of Clongowes Wood College. Map 1.1.

AUGHRIM ("The Dead": 190)
A village in Co. Galway near Ballinasloe. The ballad, "The Lass of Aughrim", reminds Gretta Conroy of her life in Galway.

AUNGIER STREET ("Ivy Day": 111)
This street was part of the Royal Exchange Ward for municipal elections. Map 5.24.

BAGGOT STREET ("Two Gallants": 46, "A Painful Case": 99)
Maps 3.16 and 5.24.

BAIRD'S STONE CUTTING WORKS (*PORTRAIT*: 176)
Todd and Baird, The Talbot Engineering Works, 15-27 Talbot Place. Map 3.15.

BALBRIGGAN ("The Dead": 169)
A coastal town nineteen miles north of Dublin. Map 1.1.

BALLAST OFFICE ("Counterparts": 85, "Grace": 141)
The Ballast Board was established to improve the port and harbour of Dublin and to that end was licensed to sell ballast. In 1786 it was replaced by the Corporation for Preserving and Improving Dublin and again in 1867 by the Port and Docks Board, who took over the Ballast Office at 19 and 20 Westmoreland Street. Map 5.26.

BALLSBRIDGE ("Clay": 90)
A suburb of Dublin one and a half miles south-east of the city centre where Ball's Bridge crosses the River Dodder. It is the location of the Dublin-by-Lamplight Laundry and the Royal Dublin Society Showgrounds. Maps 7.32 and 7.33.

BALLYHOURA HILLS (*PORTRAIT*: 182)
The foothills of the Ballyhoura Mountains in Co. Cork, about thirty miles north of Cork City. The village of Ballyhoura is located two miles north of Buttevant (Co. Cork) and ten miles south of Kilmallock (Co. Limerick).

THE BANK (*PORTRAIT*: 96, "After the Race'" 40)
The Bank of Ireland at College Green was constructed in 1725 and served as Ireland's parliament building until the Act of Union (1800) brought Ireland under the direct rule of the English parliament. After a scheme to connect it by underground tunnel to Trinity College was abandoned, the Bank of Ireland purchased the building from the government for £40,000. Maps 4.17, 5.24.

BARE CHEERLESS HOUSE (*PORTRAIT*: 66)
14 Fitzgibbon Street, off Mountjoy Square. At the beginning of 1893, the Joyce family moved here from 23 Carysfort Avenue, Blackrock. Map 2.7.

BARNARDO's (*PORTRAIT*: 97)
J.M. Barnardo and Sons, Court Furriers and Mantle Manufacturers, 108 Grafton Street. Map 6.30.

BARRACKS ("Counterparts": 88)
Beggar's Bush Infantry Barracks, corner of Haddington Road and Shelbourne Road. Map 3.16.

BELVEDERE COLLEGE (*PORTRAIT*: 71)

5-6 Great Denmark Street. James Joyce attended this Jesuit school from April 6, 1893, until June 1898. Map 2.7.

BEWLEY'S ("A Little Cloud": 74)
Charles Bewley and Company, tea and coffee merchant, 13 Great George's Street South. Map 5.25.

BLACK EAGLE ("Ivy Day": 114)
Joyce places this fictitious bar, suggesting the eighteenth-century Eagle Tavern where the "Hell-Fire Club" met, at 21 Grafton Street where Joseph Farrell kept a pub at the time. Map 6.30.

BLACKROCK (*PORTRAIT*: 60)
Once a fashionable resort, in Joyce's day Blackrock was a prosperous suburb of Dublin. The family occupied a house at 23 Carysfort Avenue, just west of Main Street and south of Blackrock (People's) Park. Before the Reformation Blackrock and nearby Monkstown were the property of the great St Mary's Abbey, and the village also had associations with the Earls of Clonmell and Cloncurry and Lord Edward Fitzgerald who appear elsewhere in this text. Map 1.1 and 1.5.

BOARDING HOUSE ("The Boarding House": 56)
The only boarding house on Hardwicke Street during the years Joyce knew Dublin was the 'Waverley' at 4 Hardwicke Street on the corner of Frederick Court. Map 6.31.

BODENSTOWN (*PORTRAIT*: 20)
Between Sallins and Clane in Co. Kildare, the Bodenstown Church is the burial place of Wolfe Tone. Map 1.4.

BOG OF ALLEN ("The Dead": 201)
An extensive bogland lying twenty miles west of Dublin in counties Kildare and Offaly, roughly between Tullamore and Naas. Map 1.1.

BOOTMAKER ON ORMOND QUAY ("A Mother": 125)
There was no bootmaker on Ormond Quay at the time "A Mother" takes place; however, a Michael Kearney kept a bootmaker's shop at 23 Wexford Street (just west of Harcourt Street: Map 12). Mr Joseph Reidy, on whose family the Kearneys in this story are based, lived at 15 Mountjoy Street. Map 6.31.

BRIDGE OVER THE TOLKA (*PORTRAIT:* 162)
Drumcondra bridge where Drumcondra Road Lower crosses the Tolka River. When the Joyce family lived at 2 Millbourne Villas (on Millbourne Lane) in 1894, Joyce passed the statue of the Virgin Mary here on the south-west side of the bridge. Map 3.12.

BROWN THOMAS'S ("A Mother": 127)
Silk mercers, milliners, costumiers, mantle-makers and general drapers, 15-17 Grafton Street. Map 5.26.

BUCKINGHAM STREET ("Araby": 30)
Map 4.20.

THE BULL (*PORTRAIT*: 164)
The North Bull is one of two islands thrown up in Dublin Bay by the action of the sea tides and the currents of the Tolka and the Liffey. The Bull was the smaller of the two islands, but survived its sister, whose sands were carried away at low tide by local farmers for use in their fields. It is connected to the mainland at Clontarf by the Bull bridge. The strand where Stephen sees the wading girl is on the east side of the island. Map. 3.14.

BUTTEVANT (*PORTRAIT*: 182)
A town in Co. Cork, six miles north of Mallow and twelve miles south of Kilmallock in Co. Limerick.

BYRON'S PUBLICHOUSE (*PORTRAIT*: 164)
Patrick Byron, family grocer, wine and spirit merchant and Italian warehouseman, 44 Ballybough Road. Map 3.14.

CABINTEELY ROAD (*PORTRAIT*: 37)
A road north from Bray to Dublin taken by Mr. Casey in *A Portrait* to avoid the arrest which awaited him had he taken the train. Map 1.2.

CAKE SHOP IN HENRY STREET ("Clay": 93)
Bewley's Oriental Cafe, 18-20 Henry Street, or Anne Mullen, confectioner, 37 Henry Street. Map 7.34.

CAKE SHOP NEAR THE PARKGATE ("A Painful Case": 102)
William O'Connor, confectioner, 40 Parkgate Street. Map 7.37.

CALLAN'S OF FOWNES'S STREET ("Counterparts": 85)
Callen and Murphy, solicitors, not in Fownes's Street but nearby at 23 St Andrew's Street. Map 5.24.

CANAL ("Two Gallants": 46)
The Grand Canal, south of the city centre. Map 3.16.

CANAL BANK ("An Encounter": 18)
Leaving the road at Summerhill Parade, the boy in "An Encounter" passes under the bridge which crosses the Royal Canal at that point and then goes along the canal bank beside the trees of Charleville Mall as far as the Newcomen Bridge at the North Strand Road. Map 4.21.

CANAL BRIDGE (*PORTRAIT*: 207)
Leeson Street Bridge where Leeson Street crosses the Grand Canal. Map 3.16.

CANAL BRIDGE ("An Encounter": 17)
Newcomen Bridge where North Strand Road crosses the Royal Canal. Map 4.21.

CANAL BRIDGE ("Clay": 94)
Binn's Bridge where Drumcondra Road Lower crosses the Royal Canal. Map 7.35.

CAPAL STREET ("A Little Cloud": 66)
Map 5.25.

CARRICKMINES (*PORTRAIT*: 63)
A rural area four miles south of Blackrock. Map 1.2.

CARYSFORT AVENUE (*PORTRAIT*: 60)
In 1892 the Joyce family moved from Martello Terrace in Bray to "Leoville", the house at 23 Carysfort Avenue, Blackrock. Aubrey Mills, who in *A Portrait* helps Stephen to found a gang of adventurers in the avenue, is probably a fictitious name, since no Mills appear listed for Carysfort Avenue or the surrounding area in the city directories or tax records for these years. Map 1.5.

THE CASTLE ("Ivy Day": 113)
Dublin Castle, the royal seat of government in Ireland since 1560, was the town residence of the Lord Lieutenant of Ireland. Its offices housed, among others, the Metropolitan Police and the Ulster King at Arms Office. Map 5.25.

CASTLE IN BLACKROCK (*PORTRAIT*: 63)
Probably the ornamental embattled structure which surmounts the reefs behind Blackrock House (about one-half mile north of the Seapoint Martello Tower). This was the scene of the famous wreck of the *Prince of Wales* in 1807. Map 1.5.

CASTLETOWNROCHE (*PORTRAIT*: 182)
A village eleven miles east of Buttevant in Co. Cork.

CATHEDRAL STREET ("A Mother": 126)
The Pro-Cathedral is located on the corner of Marlborough and Cathedral Streets. Map 7.34.

CATHOLIC WINE MERCHANT'S OFFICE ("The Boarding House": 59)
Joyce seems to have had W. and A. Gilbey, wine merchants, in mind. Their office was located at 58 Dorset Street Upper just below the boarding house. Map 6.31.

THE CHAINS ("Two Gallants": 49)
A large-link, black, decorative chain surrounding the four sides of Stephen's Green, it separated the footpath from the roadway. Map 5.24.

CHAPELIZOD ("A Painful Case": 98)
A village three and a half miles west of O'Connell Bridge, in Joyce's day it was a small community of 255 houses located on the banks of the Liffey. It is said to have derived its name from La belle Izod (Iseult), daughter of Aengus, King of Ireland. Maps 7.37 and 7.38.

CHRISTIAN BROTHERS ("Ivy Day:": 109)
At the time of the story "Ivy Day" there were twelve schools for boys under the control of the Catholic religious Order of Christian Brothers with a total enrollment of 7100 pupils. There were only three schools, however, in the city proper: the school at North Richmond Street (enrolment 2000), one at Westland Row (900), and a third at Synge and Francis Streets (1100).

CHRISTIAN BROTHERS' SCHOOL ("Araby": 25)
This school, established in 1828, is located on the corner of Richmond Place and North Richmond Street. Joyce attended the school for a short time in the spring of 1893 before entering Belvedere College in April of that year. Map 4.20.

CHURCH STREET CHAPEL (*PORTRAIT*: 141)
Capuchin Church of St Mary of the Angels on Church Street. Map 2.10.

CITY HALL ("Two Gallants": 53)
Located on Cork Hill at the end of Parliament Street, the building had formerly been the Royal Exchange (until 1852). Like the Rotunda, it was the scene of Volunteer activities in the 1780s, and during the Rising of 1798 it was used as a barracks and torture

chamber by government troops. Later, criminals were scourged on its steps. Map 5.24.

CITY MARKETS ("Two Gallants": 53)
South City Market located off Great George's Street South. The entrance was narrower than it is today, but then as now it is located between Exchequer Street and Fade Street. Map 5.24.

CITY OF DUBLIN HOSPITAL ("A Painful Case": 104)
Royal City of Dublin Hospital, 16-18 Upper Baggot Street. Map 3.16.

CLANE (*PORTRAIT:* 18)
A village four miles north of Sallins on the road to Clongowes Wood College. The village probably originated with a Celtic ecclesiastical establishment and later served a Franciscan Abbey founded by the Anglo-Normans. Its position on the border of the English Pale lent it an importance it might not have otherwise achieved. Historically, it is associated with first-century saga of King Mesgegra, King of Leinster, and Queen Baun, and, much later, with the 1798 Rising. Map 1.4.

CLONGOWES WOOD COLLEGE (*PORTRAIT:* 15)
Jesuit school for boys founded in 1814 at Castle Browne in Co. Kildare. Joyce attended Clongowes from 1888 to 1891. Map 1.4 and Fig. 1.

CLONLIFFE ROAD (*PORTRAIT:* 80)
It was here that Joyce was pummelled and pushed against a barbed-wired fence for his persistant defence of Lord Byron. Map 3.12.

CLONTARF CHAPEL (*PORTRAIT:* 164)
Roman Catholic Church of the Visitation at 10-11 Fairview Strand and Philipsburgh Avenue. Map 3.14.

COLLEGE ("An Encounter": 17)
Belvedere College, 5-6 Great Denmark Street. Joyce attended this Jesuit school from 6 April, 1893 to June 1898. Map 4.20 and Fig. 2.

COLLEGE OF SURGEONS ("Two Gallants": 53)
Royal College of Surgeons, 123 St Stephen's Green West. The clock which Lenehan consults in "Two Gallants" was over the main entrance. Map 5.24.

COMMITTEE ROOM ("Ivy Day": 109)
Apparently Joyce had 15 Wicklow Street in mind, a building listed in *Thom's* as Central Chambers. The building was occupied essentially by solicitors' offices in 1903. Map 6.30.

CONVENT ("Araby": 27)
Sisters of Charity Convent and girls' school located behind the St Francis Xavier Church on Gardiner Street. Map 4.20.

CORK (*PORTRAIT:* 86)
Cork was the family home of John Joyce before he, like many other Cork men, left the city for Dublin. Father and son revisited Cork in 1894 to dispose of the last of the elder Joyce's property. Map 2.9.

CORK HILL (*PORTRAIT:* 220)
The street directly in front of City Hall leading to Parliament Street, Dame Street, and the Castle gates. Map 5.25.

CORLESS'S ("A Little Cloud": 66)
The Burlington Hotel, 26-27 St Andrew's Street and 6 Church Lane. During the time Stephen refers to it as "Underdone's" in *A Portrait* it was called the Burlington Hotel and Oyster House and was owned by Thomas Corless. In 1903 it was purchased by the Jammett Brothers who changed its name to the Burlington Hotel and Restaurant and altered its character so that *Thom's* lists it after that year as a "high-class French restaurant". Map 5.25.

CROSBIE AND ALLEYNE ("Counterparts": 79)
C.W. Alleyne, solicitor, 24 Dame Street, and Collis and Ward, solicitors, 31 Dame Street, provide the basis for the fictitious Crosbie and Alleyne. Map 5.26.

CUSTOM HOUSE (*PORTRAIT:* 66)
Located on Customhouse Quay east of O'Connell Bridge, it was constructed on reclaimed slobland after considerable trouble and expense in 1791. Map 2.7.

DAIRY ON NORTH STRAND ROAD (*PORTRAIT*: 177)
Kelly's Dairy, 152 North Strand Road, just north of Newcomen Bridge on the east side of the street. Map 3.15.

DAME STREET ("After the Race": 40; "Two Gallants": 46)
Map 5.24.

DAN ("The Dead": 192)
Statue of Daniel O'Connell located in Lower Sackville (O'Connell) Street just across O'Connell Bridge. Map 3.15.

DAN BURKE's ("A Painful Case": 99)
Daniel Burke, publican, 50 Lower Baggot Street. Map 3.16.

DARK MUDDY LANES ("Araby": 25)
Lanes of Richmond Parade and Cotts Crescent behind the houses on North Richmond Street. Map 4.19.

DAVY BYRNE'S ("Counterparts": 84)
David Byrne, wine and spirit merchant, 21 Duke Street. Map 5.26.

DAWSON STREET ("Ivy Day": 117)
Part of the Royal Exchange Ward for municipal elections. Ward did not have his office here as "Ivy Day" suggests, but on Clare Street. Map 5.24.

THE DISTILLERY ("The Sisters": 17; "A Painful Case": 98)
The Dublin and Chapelizod Distilling Company (later the Phoenix Park Distillery) located on the River Liffey on the north side of the Lucan Road and just above the Chapelizod Bridge. John Joyce served as secretary of the distillery in 1877, losing £500 he had invested when one of the partners embezzled the company into bankruptcy. Before becoming the disused distillery of "A Painful Case" the building had been a convent, a soldiers' barracks and a flax factory. Map 7.38.

THE DODDER ("An Encounter": 19)
Arising near Glencree in south Co. Dublin, the Dodder flows north-east through Ballsbridge to Ringsend where it joins the Liffey as it empties into Dublin Bay. Map 1.1.

DOLLYMOUNT (*PORTRAIT*: 165)
Dollymount lies east of Fairview and Clontarf on Dublin Bay. It is here that Stephen turns and sets out over the plank bridge to the Bull. Map 3.14.

DORSET STREET ("Two Gallants": 45)
Map 6.31.

DOWNES'S CAKE SHOP ("Clay": 93)
Sir Joseph Downes, merchant baker, confectioner, 5-6 North Earl Street. Map 7.34.

DRAPERY SHOP ("The Sisters": 9)
Joyce has the Misses Monaghan Drapery at 109 Great Britain (Parnell) Street in mind. Map 4.20 and Fig. 3.

DRUMCONDRA ("Clay": 90)
Maria's journey to Drumcondra in "Clay" actually takes her to the townland of Clonliffe West, lying between the Tolka River and the Royal Canal and west of the Drumcondra Road. Through popular usage, however, the Drumcondra Road, beginning just north of the Royal Canal, came to be confused with the district of Drumcondra and thus Drumcondra usurped the place of Clonliffe as the name of the area. In 1894 the Joyce family lived north of the Tolka on Millbourne Lane within the true boundaries of Drumcondra district. Maps 7.35 and 3.13.

DUBLIN-BY-LAMPLIGHT LAUNDRY ("Clay": 92)
The Dublin-by-Lamplight Institute with laundry attached, 35 Ballsbridge Terrace. Map 7.33.

DUBLIN MOUNTAINS (*PORTRAIT*: 62)
Map 1.2.

DUBLIN UNIVERSITY (*PORTRAIT*: 175 "After the Race": 39)
Burn-chapel Whaley's old mansion at 86 St Stephen's Green was bought in 1853 by Cardinal Cullen for the Catholic University of Ireland. John Henry Newman became its first rector, but left after five years, disappointed by the difficulties with which he had been faced and his resulting lack of progress. In 1883 it was taken over by the Jesuits. The school struggled along under the aegis of the Royal University and was still very much a second-class institution when Joyce attended classes there, although several of his classmates distinguished themselves both at the college and afterwards. Dublin University, Royal University and Catholic University are, as Joyce uses them, all names for University College, Dublin. Map 3.16.

DUKE'S LAWN (*PORTRAIT*: 215, "Two Gallants": 51)
The lawn of Leinster House, once the Duke of Leinster's residence. Leinster House was, in Joyce's day, the headquarters of the Royal Dublin Society and the Department of Agriculture. The lawn or 'garden front' is located on Merrion Square West, the 'principal front' on Kildare Street. Maps 3.16, 5.24.

DUNN'S OF D'OLIER STREET (*PORTRAIT*: 29)
Joseph Dunn, poulterer and fishmonger, 26 D'Olier Street. Map 3.15.

EARLSFORT TERRACE ("A Painful Case": 101)

The Royal University, established in 1879 as an examining body for the Dublin University, occupied the buildings of the old Dublin Exhibition on Earlsfort Terrace. Besides lecture rooms and offices, there were two large halls here used by permission of the Royal University for concerts of the Orchestral Society. Map 3.16.

EARL STREET ("Two Gallants": 48)

North Earl Street off Sackville (O'Connell) Street at the Pillar. The reference in "Two Gallants" is to Earl Street as a frequently used entrance via Talbot Street to 'Monto' ("Nighttown"), Dublin's notorious prostitute district. Map 2.9.

EATING HOUSE IN GEORGE'S STREET ("A Painful Case": 99)

Joyce's description points to Fleming's Restaurant and Dining Rooms, 1 Great George's Street South. Map 5.25.

EGAN'S ("Two Gallants": 53)

John Egan, the 'Oval' Pub, 78 Abbey Street Middle. Map 5.24.

ELY PLACE ("Two Gallants": 53)

Map 5.24.

EUSTACE STREET ("Counterparts": 81)

Map 5.26.

EVELINE'S HOUSE ("Eveline": 32)

The Eveline of this story is based on Eveline Thornton who lived near the Joyce family at 42 Richmond Avenue in Fairview. The neighbourhood he describes is based on that address. Map 3.14.

FAIRVIEW SLOBLANDS (*PORTRAIT*: 176)

The tidelands at the mouth of the Tolka around Annesley Bridge. This area has been reclaimed and is now Fairview Park. The sight of the Tolka flowing over the silt and under the middle arch of the Northern Railway bridge at low tide reminds Stephen of Newman's "silverveined prose". Map 3.14.

FARRINGTON'S HOUSE ("Counterparts": 88)

16 Shelbourne Road. Map 3.16.

FEUDAL ARCH OF KING'S INNS ("A Little Cloud": 66)

The arched, stone entrance at the rear of King's Inns, located at the top of Henrietta Street. Map. 5.25.

FIFTEEN ACRES ("The Dead": 182)

Actually a 150-acre area of the 1700-acre Phoenix Park lying north of Chapelizod Gate and about one mile west of the Wellington Monument. Map 7.37.

FINDLATER'S CHURCH (*PORTRAIT*: 160)

The Abbey Presbyterian Church was built in 1862-64 at the expense of Alexander Findlater. It dominates the corner of Rutland (Parnell) Square and North Frederick Street. Map 6.31.

FIRST GATE OF PHOENIX PARK ("A Painful Case": 106)

Chapelizod Gate is the first gate to Phoenix Park for Mr Duffy as he walks towards Dublin from the public

house in Chapelizod. Map 7.37.

FLEET STREET ("Counterparts": 84)

Map 5.26.

FOGARTY'S ("Grace": 143)

Fogarty's grocery was not located on the Glasnevin Road as "Grace" says but Patrick Fogarty, family grocer and wine and spirit merchant, was located at 35 Glengariff Parade, two doors from the Joyce family residence of 1901. Map 5.27.

FOSTER PLACE (*PORTRAIT*: 96)

A *cul-de-sac* next to the west entrance of the Bank of Ireland. Map 5.25.

FOURCOURTS ("The Dead": 191)

The Courts of Justice on King's Inns (now Inn's) Quay. Map 6.29.

FREEMAN'S JOURNAL ("A Mother": 132; "Grace": 146)

The extensive offices of *The Freeman's Journal* lay between North Prince's Street and Abbey Street Middle. Map 7.34.

GAIETY ("The Dead": 179)

The Gaiety Theatre, 46-49 South King Street. Map 5.24.

GALWAY ("The Dead": 198)

A major city on the west coast of Ireland. Nora Barnacle, Joyce's wife, came from Galway and while there knew Michael Bodkin, the model for Michael Furey in "The Dead".

GARDINER STREET (*PORTRAIT*: 161)

Gardiner Street Upper. St Francis Xavier's Church and the Jesuit House are located here. Map 3.12.

GARDINER STREET CHURCH ("An Encounter": 16, "Grace": 157)

The Jesuit Church of St Francis Xavier. Map 5.27.

GEORGE'S CHURCH ("The Boarding House": 58)

St George's Church at the head of Hardwicke Street, built by Sir John Eccles, Lord Mayor of Dublin in 1710, for his Protestant tenants. Map 6.31.

GEORGE'S STREET (*PORTRAIT*: 86)

Great George's Street North, between the front of Belvedere House and Marlborough Street. Map 2.7.

GEORGE'S STREET ("Two Gallants": 53; "A Painful Case": 99)

Great George's Street South. Map 5.24.

GLASNEVIN ROAD ("Grace": 142)

There was no road of this name. Joyce refers to the Phibsborough Road north of the North Circular Road. The Joyce family lived at 7 St Peter's Terrace, off Phibsborough, in 1902. Map 5.27.

GOATSTOWN ROAD (*PORTRAIT*: 62)

Map 1.2.

GRAFTON STREET (*PORTRAIT*: 184, "After the Race": 40; "Two Gallants"; "Grace": 141)

Between Trinity College and St Stephen's Green. Maps 3.15, 5.24.

GRANTHAM STREET (*PORTRAIT*: 180)

South-west of the university on St Stephen's Green

between Camden Street and Heytesbury Street. Stephen visited Davin here.

GRATTAN BRIDGE ("A Little Cloud": 67)
Located where Capel Street crosses the Liffey. Map 5.25.

GREAT BRITAIN STREET ("The Sisters": 9)
Now Parnell Street. Map 4.20.

THE GREEN ("Two Gallants": 54)
St Stephen's Green. Map 5.24.

GRESHAM HOTEL ("The Dead": 164)
21-22 Upper Sackville (O'Connell) Street. Map 7.34.

GREYSTONES ("The Dead": 126)
A resort town on the east coast of Ireland, sixteen miles south of Dublin. Map 6.28.

HADDINGTON ROAD CHURCH ("The Dead": 160)
Mary Jane, the niece of the Misses Morkan in "The Dead", is the organist in the Catholic church on Haddington Road where she also gives lessons to children of the "better-class families". Map 3.16.

HARCOURT STREET (*PORTRAIT*: 202)
Continues south from the southwest corner of St Stephen's Green. Harcourt Street Station was the Terminus for the Dublin, Wicklow and Wexford Railway on which Cranly traveled back and forth to his home. It is located between Harcourt Street and Hatch Street. Map 3.16.

HARDWICKE STREET ("The Boarding House": 56)
Map 6.31.

THE HEAD (*PORTRAIT*: 28)
Bray Head, one mile south along the Strand Road from Martello Terrace, Bray. Map 1.1.

HENRIETTA STREET ("A Little Cloud": 66)
Once the residence of the greatest land-owners in Dublin, the street is little more than tenements by the time Little Chandler walks there. Map 5.25.

HICKEY'S ("The Dead": 170)
Michael Hickey, bookseller, 8 Bachelor's Walk. Map 5.24.

HILL AT INCHICORE ("After the Race": 38)
Map 7.37.

HILL OF HOWTH (*PORTRAIT*: 170) ("Eveline": 34)
Howth, located on a peninsula eight miles northeast of Dublin city-centre, is dominated by Ben of Howth rising 500 feet above sea level. The Joyce family often took picnics here as well as to Bull Island. The peninsula is clearly visible to Stephen from the Bull Wall which lies three miles across the water to the west. Map 1.1.

HILL OF LYONS (*PORTRAIT*: 40)
The Hill of Lyons was on the Cloncurry estate, seven miles east of Clane between the Liffey River and the Dublin to Cork Railway line. Map 1.4. In Dante's Hell, the sins of violence (or Bestility) are called "the sins of the Lion." See Dante's L'Inferno cantos IX-XXII with reference to the "smugging" incident.

HILL OF RUTLAND SQUARE ("Two Gallants": 45)
Rutland (Parnell) Square East, below Dorset Street.

Map 6.31.

HOLYHEAD (*PORTRAIT*: 250)
Holyhead, Wales, was the destination of ferries crossing the Irish Sea from Dublin's North Wall Quay (Joyce left for France *via* this route), or from Kingstown (Dun Laoghaire).

HOPKINS' CORNER (*PORTRAIT*: 177)
Hopkins and Hopkins, jewellers, goldsmiths, silversmiths, and watchmakers, 1 Lower Sackville (O'Connell) Street. Map 3.15.

HOTEL GROUNDS (*PORTRAIT*: 43)
Royal Marine Hotel, Strand Road, Bray. Map 1.3.

HOWTH ("A Mother": 126)
See Hill of Howth.

HUCKSTER'S SHOP IN RINGSEND ("An Encounter": 19)
William Grimley, family grocer, 39 Thorncastle Street. Map 4.22.

HUME STREET ("Two Gallants": 49)
Map 2.10.

INCHICORE ("After the Race": 38)
Map 7.37.

IRISH TIMES ("Grace": 146)
31 Westmoreland Street. Map 5.24.

IRISHTOWN ("The Sisters": 14)
The area south of Ringsend, one and a half miles east of the city centre. Map 4.18.

JACOB'S BISCUIT FACTORY (*PORTRAIT*: 220)
William Jacob and Co., steam biscuit bakery, 5-12 Peter's Row and 19-21, 28-29, and 50 Bishop Street, just west of Aungier Street. Map 5.24.

JESUIT HOUSE (*PORTRAIT*: 161)
Residence for the Jesuit Order beside St Francis Xavier Church on Gardiner Street Upper. Map 3.12.

JOE'S HOUSE ("Clay": 49)
55 St Brigid's Road Lower. Map 7.35.

JOHNNY RUSH'S ("The Sisters": 14)
John Rush, carriage and cab proprietor, 10 Gregg's Lane (Findlater Place). Map 4.20.

JONES'S ROAD (*PORTRAIT*: 82)
Map 3.12.

KAVANAGH'S ("Ivy Day": 115)
Kavanagh's Wine Rooms, on the corner of Parliament Street and Essex Gate. Map 5.25.

KILDARE (*PORTRAIT*: 25)
Co. Kildare, the location of Clongowes Wood College. Map 1.1.

KILDARE STREET (*PORTRAIT*: 237 "Two Gallants": 49) Maps, 3.16, 5.24.

KILMALLOCK (*PORTRAIT*: 182)
A town in Co. Limerick eighteen miles south of Limerick City and twelve miles north of Buttevant in Co. Cork.

KING BILLY'S STATUE ("The Dead": 187)
An equestrian statue of William of Orange which in

Joyce's day stood before Trinity College in College Green. Frequently vandalized it was finally removed in 1929. Two sections from the plinth are preserved at the Dublin Civic Museum, William Street. Map 5.25.

KINGSBRIDGE STATION (*PORTRAIT:* 86 "A Painful Case": 107)
Now Heuston Station, trains west for Sallins and Cork would have left from here. Map 7.37.

KING'S INNS ("A Little Cloud": 64)
King's Inns faces west onto Constitution Hill with a rear entrance through a stone gate into Henrietta Street. The *Dictionary of Dublin* for 1906 called this entrance "prison-like and depressing". One section of the building was controlled by the Society of King's Inns, a semi-official body whose function it was to regulate the profession of the Bar in Dublin. This section contained a dining-hall, a 'prerogative court' and a law library. The other section was the office for the registry of deeds. Maps 5.25 and 2.10.

KINGSTOWN STATION AND HARBOUR ("After the Race": 42)
The Royal Mail Packet Station of Kingstown Harbour. The name was changed from Dunleary in 1821 to commemorate King George IV's departure from this port. It is now called Dun Laoghaire. Map 7.36.

LANE BEHIND THE TERRACE (*PORTRAIT:* 175)
The lane behind Royal Terrace (now Inverness) which ran along beside the east wall of St Vincent's Lunatic Asylum. In 1900 the Joyce family lived at 8 Royal Terrace. Map 3.14.

LANE OFF GRAFTON STREET ("Grace": 138)
Adam's Court. The Empire Buffet occupied the premises at numbers 1, 2 and 3. In *Ulysses*, Bloom passes Adam's Court and sees Bob Doran "sloping" into the Empire Pub "on his annual bend", the result, perhaps, of his forced marriage consequent to the events recounted in "The Boarding House". Map 5.26.

LARRAS (*PORTRAIT:* 245)
Laragh, Co. Wicklow, lies about ten miles directly south of Sallygap. The shortest way between the two, however, is to go east and then back west thereby avoiding the mountains in between. Map 1.1.

LEE RIVER (*PORTRAIT:* 94)
Rising in the south-west of Ireland above Bantry Bay, the Lee flows east into Cork City where the construction of quays has divided it into a north and a south channel. The river flows into the sea at Queenstown (now Cobh). Map 2.9.

LEESON PARK (*PORTRAIT:* 247)
Map 3.16.

LEOPARDSTOWN (*PORTRAIT:* 191)
Leopardstown Race Course, six miles south of Dublin city centre, beside the Fox Rock railway station. The area was originally called 'Leperstown' because it was

the location of a leper's hospital. Map 1.2.

LEOVILLE, SYDNEY PARADE ("A Painful Case": 105)
The House called "Leoville" on Sydney Parade Avenue is imaginary. Joyce takes the name from the house at 23 Carysfort Avenue where his family lived in 1892. The name "Sinico" is borrowed from a composer Joyce knew in Trieste. Sydney Parade Avenue and Station is located south-east of Ballsbridge, three miles from Dublin city centre. Map 7.32.

LIFFEY LOAN BANK ("Grace": 147)
Joyce is apparently referring to the Central Bank, 22 Fownes's Street. Map 5.26.

LIFFEY RIVER ("An Encounter": 19, *PORTRAIT:* 94)
Rising eight and a half miles west of Bray at Sallygap, the Liffey flows west and then north, passing Clongowes Wood College in Co. Kildare, then east through Chapelizod and the centre of Dublin, emptying into Dublin Bay. Map 1.1.

LOWER MOUNT STREET (*PORTRAIT:* 210)
Map 3.16.

MAGAZINE HILL ("A Painful Case": 107)
Magazine Fort, an ammunition depot used at the turn of the century by the British garrison in Dublin, is located on the south-eastern edge of Phoenix Park on top of a rise known as Thomas's Hill. Legend has it that this is Isolde's Hill and the location of Isolde's Well. The magazine is just a mile along the winding road which leads from Chapelizod Gate to Islandbridge Gate. From the top of Magazine Hill the wall which marks the southern boundary of the park is clearly visible though it is hidden by rolling ground from those who stay on the road. The River Liffey is also visible beyond the river. Map 7.37.

MALAHIDE (*PORTRAIT:* 232)
A coastal village eight miles north-east of the Dublin city centre. In *A Portrait* Stephen remembers praying in a wood near Malahide, "knowing that he stood on holy ground and in a holy hour". Joyce probably had either the castle and demense of Lord Talbot de Malahide or the village of St Doolagh in mind. The former was famous for its woods and ruined chapel containing the tomb of Richard Talbot's wife, who died in the fifteenth century. The castle, dating from 1174, contained a painting of the Nativity of Our Lord which had once been on the altar in the chapel of Holyrood Palace. The wood is located about a half-mile south of Malahide near a sharp bend in the road. St Doolagh is two miles closer to Dublin along the same road and perhaps even richer in its religious associations. St Doolagh, whose feast day is the 17th of November, gives his name to the fourteenth-century Saxon church as well as the village, and his 'bed of penance' and St Catherine's Well are located nearby. On the road between these two points are churches dedicated to St Nicholas of Tolentino, of the Augustinian Order, whose feast day is the 10th of September, and to St Nicholas of Myra, who is

honoured on the 6th of December, as well as an Old High Cross and the Well of St Werburgh, one of the patron saints of Dublin. Aside from the symbols and shrines of christian significance, it is worth noting, in view of Stephen's changing spiritual proclivities, that the ancient celts placed a large number of fine goods into wells, peat bogs, lakes and rivers, as well as in sacred groves in forests, in reverence for the water deity. The "holy ground" of which Stephen speaks may well have been sanctified to this purpose. Map 1.1.

THE MALL ("An Encounter": 18)
Charleville Mall. Map 4.21.

MALLOW (*PORTRAIT*: 87)
A town in Co. Cork, eighteen miles north of Cork City on the railway line from Dublin. Mallow lies about ninety miles by rail south west of Maryborough (Port Laoise).

MANSION HOUSE("Ivy Day": 116)
Residence of the Lord Mayor of Dublin, 19 Dawson Street. Map 5.24.

MAPLE'S HOTEL (*PORTRAIT*: 237)
23-28 Kildare Street. Map 3.16.

MARDYKE WALK (*PORTRAIT*: 89)
Promenade between the north and south channels of the River Lee in Cork. Map 2.9.

MARINE DEALER'S SHOP (*PORTRAIT*: 176)
M'Cann, Verdon, and Co., flax, hemp, twine, sail, and patent rope manufacturers, 2 Burgh Quay. Philip M'Cann, Joyce's godfather, owned this chandler's shop. Map 3.15.

MARLBOROUGH STREET ("The Boarding House": 58)
The Catholic Pro-Cathedral on the corner of Marlborough Street and Cathedral Street. Map 6.31 and 7.34.

MARYBOROUGH (*PORTRAIT*: 87)
Now Port Laoise, a town in Co. Leix on the railway line fifty miles south-west of Dublin.

MARY'S LANE ("Ivy Day": 112)
Map 6.29.

MASSEY'S ("The Dead": 170)
Edward Massey, bookseller, 6 Aston's Quay. Map 5.24.

M'AULEY'S ("Grace": 149)
Thomas M'Auley, wine and spirit merchant, 39 Dorset Street Lower. Map 5.27.

MERRION ("The Dead": 163)
Mount Merrion, a neighbourhood located about four miles south-east of Dublin city centre. John Joyce, coming from his residence in Kingstown, would have passed by here on his way to Christmas gatherings at the Misses Flynns, 15 Usher's Island. Map 7.36.

MERRION ROAD (*PORTRAIT*: 65. "Two Gallants": 51) Maps 1.2, 5.24 ("Two Gallants")
Map 1.2. (*PORTRAIT*)

MERRION SQUARE (*PORTRAIT*: 211)
Map 3.16.

MERRION STREET ("Two Gallants": 49)
Map. 5.24.

MIDLAND RAILWAY ("Grace": 146)
The Midland Great Western Railway with termini at Broadstone and 43-45 North Wall Quay. Maps 4.21 and 5.27.

THE MISSES MORKAN ("The Dead": 160)
The Misses Flynn, teachers, pianoforte and singing, 15 Usher's Island. The ground floor was occupied at the same time by M. Smith and Son, forage contractors, seed and commission merchants. Between 1865 and 1878, when Joyce's mother took lessons from them, the Misses Flynn (Mrs Lyons and Mrs Callanan) operated their school from their home at 16 Ellis Quay. Map 6.29.

MOLESWORTH STREET (*PORTRAIT*: 224)
Map 3.16.

MONKSTOWN ("The Dead": 163)
A neighbourhood located about five miles south-east of the Dublin city centre. John Joyce, from whom the character "Gabriel Conroy" is partially drawn, lived at one time at 47 Northumberland Avenue in Kingstown (Dun Laoghaire), just south of Monkstown. Map 6.36.

MORGUE (*PORTRAIT*: 86)
At the time that Stephen refers to it in *A Portrait*, the city morgue had not yet moved to 3 Store Street (where it is found in *Ulysses*) but was located on the corner of Abbey Street Old and Marlborough Street. In 1904, the morgue and the adjoining Mechanics' Institute were purchased and rebuilt to house the Abbey Theatre. Map 2.7.

MULLIGAN'S ("Counterparts": 85)
James Mulligan, publican, 8 Poolbeg Street. Map 5.26.

NAAS ROAD ("After the Race": 38)
The road from Naas (Co. Kildare) runs north-east to Dublin passing through Inchicore. As it enters Dublin it becomes in turn Kilmainham Street, James Street, Thomas Street and High Street. After passing Dublin Castle it becomes Dame Street leading to the Bank of Ireland at College Green. Maps 4.17, 1.1, and 7.37.

NASSAU STREET ("Two Gallants": 49)
Map 5.24.

NATIONAL LIBRARY (*PORTRAIT*: 215)
The national library was established in 1877 and opened in Kildare Street at ceremonies in the summer of 1890. It was a gathering place for university undergraduates, to whom special reading privileges were granted due to the inadequacy of Dublin university's library. Map 3.16.

NATIONAL THEATRE (*PORTRAIT*: 226)
On May 8, 1899, the Irish National Theatre staged its first production in the Antient Concert Rooms, 42 Great Brunswick Street. It was *The Countess Cathleen*, one half of the bill that night, which created the uproar to which Stephen alludes. At the time, however, riotous behaviour at the theatre was so

common as to be rather part of the entertainment for certain playgoers. Map 5.24.

NEWCOMBE'S COFFEEHOUSE (*PORTRAIT*: 93)

Probably Newcombe's Breakfasthouse, Cork, an establishment similar to Bewely's, which appears in Guy's *County and City of Cork Directory*, 1894.

NEWSAGENT'S ON NORTH STRAND ROAD (*POR-TRAIT*: 177)

Sarah Topham, newsagent, 35 North Strand Road, just south of Necomen Bridge on the west side of the street. Map 3.15.

NORTH STRAND ROAD (*PORTRAIT*: 176 "An Encounter": 18)

Maps 3.15, 4.21.

NORTH WALL STATION ("Eveline": 35)

The location of the Midland Railway Company of England, the Glasgow, Dublin and London Steampacket Company, the Cunard Lines and Inman Line Atlantic Steamers, and the National Steam Ship Company and Orient Line of Australian Steamers: 43-45 North Wall Quay. Map 4.21.

NUN'S ISLAND ("The Dead": 199)

Nora Barnacle, Joyce's wife and partial inspiration for "Gretta" in "The Dead", lived with her grandmother on Nun's Island in Galway city.

NUN'S MADHOUSE (*PORTRAIT*: 175)

St Vincent's Lunatic Asylum (now St Vincent's Hospital). The grounds are located at the end of Convent Avenue in Fairview. Map 3.14.

O'CLOHISSEY'S ("The Dead": 170)

M. Clohissey, bookseller, 10-11 Bedford Row. Map 5.24.

O'CONNELL BRIDGE ("Counterparts": 192)

This bridge, the focal point of Dublin now that Nelson's Pillar is gone, replaced Carlisle Bridge in 1880. Map 5.26.

O'FARRELL'S ("Ivy Day": 117)

The name for this pub is drawn from Joseph Farrell, grocer, wine and spirit merchant at 21 Grafton Street, but Joyce places it at 37 Wicklow Street, the site of another pub run at the time by Thomas O'Neill. Map 6.29.

OFFICE IN CROWE STREET ("Grace": 142)

There was no tea company office in Crowe Street, but Joyce may have had E. and C. Figgis, tea merchants, in mind; they were around the corner from Crowe Street at 10 Fownes's Street. Map 5.26.

OUGHTERARD ("The Dead": 198)

A village in the west of Ireland (Co. Galway) located sixteen miles north-west of Galway city on Lough Corrib. Both Michael Furey of "The Dead" and Michael Bodkin, his real-life progenitor, are buried in the cemetery there.

THE PARK ("A Painful Case": 102)

Phoenix Park. Maps 4.17 and 7.37.

PEMBROKE TOWNSHIP (*PORTRAIT*: 244)

Pembroke Township also included Ringsend, Merrion, Ballsbridge, Beggar's Bush, Clonskea and Sandymount, but here Joyce refers to the area between the Grand Canal and Donnybrook which was a quite beautiful suburb. Map 3.11.

PIERHEAD (*PORTRAIT*: 27)

Charles Stewart Parnell died in Brighton on October 6, 1891, and his body was returned to Ireland on October 11, arriving in the rain at Kingstown Harbour. Stephen dreams of this event at Clongowes, associating the pier at Kingstown with the one behind his home in Bray. Map 1.2.

PIGEON HOUSE ("An Encounter": 17)

The Pigeon House Fort, located about one and a quarter miles from Ringsend on the south wall of Dublin Bay, was purchased by the government for a barracks in 1814 and at one time was surrounded by heavy cannon. *Thom's Directory* for 1895 lists it as an "Armoury, Artillery Stores, Magazine, and Infantry Barracks of the Garrison". Map 4.17.

THE PILLAR ("Clay": 90)

The column dedicated to Admiral Nelson and topped by his statue was once the "heart of the Hibernian metropolis" located in the middle of Sackville (O'Connell) Street where Henry Street intersects. It formed the central hub of the city's tram system. Erected in 1808, the £6856 cost met by public subscription, it was blown up in an attempt to assert Irish nationalism. The statue's head has been salvaged and may be seen at the Dublin Civic Museum. Map 7.34.

PIM'S ("Two Gallants": 46)

Pim Brothers, wholesale and retail linen and woollen-drapers, silk mercers, leather merchants, and upholsterers, 68 and 75-88 Great George's Street South, 10-17 Exchequer Street, 17-19 Sycamore Street and 7 Dame Lane — a business with enough employees and addresses to suit Corley's purpose admirably. Map 5.24.

POLICE BARRACKS (*PORTRAIT*: 164)

Royal Irish Constabulary Barracks, 2 Fairview Strand. Map 3.14.

PORCH OF THE CLUB ("Two Gallants": 49)

The Kildare Street Club, 1-3 Kildare Street. Map 5.24.

PORT AND DOCKS ("Grace": 163)

Dublin Port and Docks Authority, successor of the Ballast Board, 19-21 Westmoreland Street. Map 5.26.

PRIVATE BANK IN BAGGOT STREET ("A Painful Case": 99)

Joyce probably had in mind the Royal Bank of Ireland since it was located at 54 Baggot Street just a few doors from Dan Burke's. Map 3.16.

PRO-CATHEDRAL ("A Mother": 126)

Catholic church located on the corner of Marlborough Street and Cathedral Street. Map 7.34.

PUBLIC HOUSE AT CHAPELIZOD ("A Painful Case": 106)

The Bridge Inn at Chapelizod Bridge. Map 7.37 and

7.38.

PUBLIC HOUSE IN DORSET STREET ("Two Gallants": 45)

Probably either Larry O'Rourke's on the corner of Dorset Street Upper and Eccles Street or Thomas M'Auley's at 39 Dorset Street Lower. There were, however, at least thirteen pubs on Dorset Street in Joyce's day. Map 5.27.

QUEEN'S COLLEGE, Cork (*PORTRAIT*: 89)

John Joyce entered Queen's College in 1867 and unsuccessfully pursued a medical course for three years, though he excelled in extracurricular activities. Twenty-seven years later, he returned there with his son, and the episode became part of Stephen's awakening in *A Portrait*. Map 2.9.

QUEENSTOWN (*PORTRAIT*: 92)

Now Cobh Harbour, Co. Cork.

REFRESHMENT BAR ("Two Gallants": 52)

There was no refreshment bar on Great Britain Street fitting the details suggested in "Two Gallants" during Joyce's years in Dublin. The closest refreshment bar to where he has Lenehan stop was the Hibernian Restaurant Room around the corner and down the street at 138 Capel Street. Map 5.24.

RINGSEND ("An Encounter": 19)

Map 4.22.

ROCK ROAD (*PORTRAIT*: 64)

Blackrock. Map 1.5.

ROTUNDA ("A Painful Case": 99, *PORTRAIT*: 249)

The domed Rotunda Hospital in Rutland (Parnell) Square was supported in part by concerts and other entertainments held in the Rotunda Rooms, which included a large concert hall. The Round Rooms (now the Ambassador) were the birthplace of the Irish Volunteers and were also used by Napper Tandy and the United Irishmen in 1796. From that time on it was the meeting place of revolutionaries — in 1848, 1867, 1882 — up to the birth of Sinn Fein there in 1905. Map 6.31.

ROYAL IRISH ACADEMY (*PORTRAIT*: 215)

The Royal Irish Academy was at 19 Dawson Street. In Chapter Five of *A Portrait* Stephen passes between Leinster House and the Metropolitan School of Art, housed in a building constructed in 1843. In 1900 it had passed from the control of the Royal Dublin Society to the Department of Agriculture and Technical Instruction. Map 3.16.

RUTLAND SQUARE ("Two Gallants": 45)

Now Parnell Square. Map 5.24.

ST CATHERINE'S CHURCH, MEATH STREET ("The Sisters": 9)

Map 6.29.

ST STEPHEN'S GREEN (*PORTRAIT*: 184)

The quarter-mile square park was first enclosed in 1670 to preserve some parkland for the residents of the growing city. The central portion was planted and lots around the perifery were distributed among some of the city's more prosperous citizens. They were not required to build, and for some time much of the south and east side was retained in agriculture and grazing. Neglected during the early 1800s, the park was renovated in 1880. The duck pond calls to mind the paragraph in Chapter Five which begins: "The park trees were heavy with rain and rain fell still and ever in the lake, lying grey like a shield. A game of swans flew there and the water and the shore beneath were fouled with their greenwhite slime." Map 3.16.

SALLINS (*PORTRAIT*: 18)

A canal village twenty miles (one hour) by train from Kingsbridge (Heuston) Station, Dublin, and about four miles south of Clongowes Wood College. Maps 1.1 and 5.25.

SALLYGAP (*PORTRAIT*: 245)

Eight and a half miles west of Bray and twelve miles south of Dublin, Sally Gap is a passage through the Wicklow Mountains and the meeting place of the two sources of the Liffey. Map 1.1.

SANDYFORD (*PORTRAIT*: 62)

A village about three and a half miles south-west of Blackrock and two miles south of Dundrum. Map 1.2.

SANDYMOUNT TRAM ("Counterparts": 87)

From the Pillar to Sandymount via O'Connell Bridge, Westmoreland Street, Nassau Street, Mount Street Lower, Northumberland Road, Haddington Road, Bath Avenue and Tritonville Road. Map 5.23.

SCOTCH HOUSE ("Counterparts": 85)

Public House at 6 and 7 Burgh Quay at the corner of Hawkins Street. Map 5.26.

SÉGOUIN'S HOTEL ("After the Race": 40)

The Shelbourne Hotel, 27-32 Stephen's Green North. Map 5.24.

SHANNON WAVES ("The Dead": 201)

The River Shannon flows into the Atlantic on the west coast of Ireland between counties Kerry and Clare.

SHELBOURNE HOTEL ("Two Gallants": 51)

27-32 St Stephen's Green North. Map 5.24.

SHELBOURNE ROAD ("Counterparts": 87)

William Murray, Joyce's uncle and part of the basis for Farrington in "Counterparts", lived at 16 Shelbourne Road after leaving North Strand Road. Joyce had a room at 60 Shelbourne Road with the M'Kernan family. Map 3.16.

SIR PATRICK DUN'S HOSPITAL (*PORTRAIT*: 204)

Between Mount Street Lower and Grand Canal Street Lower. Map 3.16.

SIR PHILIP CRAMPTON (*PORTRAIT:* 214)

Memorial bust of Sir Philip Crampton located in Joyce's time at the junction of College Street with Great Brunswick (Pearse) Street and D'Olier Street. It supported three drinking fountains in its base and an inscription dedicating it to "health and usefulness". The *Dictionary of Dublin* (1906) notes that it was popularly known as the "Cauliflower", a reference to the stone foliage rising above the bust. The statue was said to mark the site of the ancient Danish Long Stone or Steyne. Map 3.15.

SKERRIES ("A Mother": 126)

A seaside village about nineteen miles north of Dublin and a popular summer resort and bathing-place for Dubliners. Map 1.1.

SLAB TO THE MEMORY OF WOLFE TONE (*PORTRAIT*: 184)

On August 15, 1898, the foundation stone of a monument to Wolfe Tone and the United Irishmen was laid in St Stephen's Green at the top of Grafton Street. Joyce and his father attended the ceremony. Map 3.15.

SMOOTHING IRON ("An Encounter": 18)

A bathing-place off the East Wall or Wharf Road located at the end of Merchant's Street. A wharf constructed here in 1800 for bathers had a stone platform used by divers. Its shape suggested a smoothing iron and the place became known by this name. Map 4.21.

SOUTH CIRCULAR ("Two Gallants": 47)

South Circular Road. Map 5.23.

SOUTH TERRACE (*PORTRAIT*: 92)

The location of John Joyce's boyhood home in Cork. Map 2.9.

THE SQUARE (*PORTRAIT*: 66)

Mountjoy Square. Map 2.7.

STARCH MILL IN BACK LANE ("The Dead": 186)

56, 58, 59 and 60 Back Lane. Map. 6.29.

STAR OF THE SEA CHURCH ("Grace": 143)

Located on the corner of Leahy's Terrace and the Tritonville Road in Sandymount. Map 5.23.

THE STATION ("Araby": 30)

Amien's Street (Connolly) Railway Station. Map 4.20.

STATUTE OF THE NATIONAL POET (*PORTRAIT*: 180)

The statue of the poet Thomas Moore located at the junction of Westmoreland and College Streets. The *Dictionary of Dublin* (1906) calls it "the strangely ungraceful figure intended to perpetuate the memory of Ireland's most graceful poet". Joyce calls Moore a "Firbolg in the borrowed cloak of a Milesian." Briefly, the Firbolgs were a pastoral people who, along with a second group of settlers in Ireland — the Tuatha de Danann, were subjugated by the warrior Milesians (c. 1000 BC), who believed themselves destined to live and rule in Ireland: a situation reminiscent of that which embroiled the Irish and the English. Moore put on the cloak of his conquerers and spent his life among them. Map 3.15.

STILLORGAN (*PORTRAIT*: 62)

In Joyce's time a picturesque village one and a half miles south-west of Blackrock and two miles south-east of Dundrum. Map 1.2.

STONEY BATTER ("The Dead": 160)

Literally, the 'road of stones', it once formed part of the road from Tara by the sea to Wicklow, crossing the Liffey at the Ford of Hurdles (*Atha Cliath*) where the Father Matthew Bridge now crosses. At the time the Misses Morkan would have lived there, Stoneybatter extended only the short distance between Manor Street and King Street North. Map 6.29.

STRADBOOK ROAD (*PORTRAIT*: 63)

Map 1.2.

SUB—SHERIFF'S OFFICE ("Grace": 146)

2 King's Inns Quay (now Inn's Quay). Map 6.29.

SUFFOLK STREET CORNER ("Ivy Day": 115)

The corner of Suffolk and Grafton Streets. Map 6.30.

SUNDAY'S WELL (*PORTRAIT*: 94)

A suburban district in Cork city. Site of a holy well known for the curative powers of its water — particularly for the eyes. Map 2.9.

SYDNEY PARADE STATION ("A Painful Case": 104)

A railway station south of Ballsbridge on the Dublin-Blackrock-Bray line. Map 7.32.

TALBOT PLACE (*PORTRAIT*: 176)

Map 3.15.

TEMPLE BAR ("Counterparts": 84)

The narrow alleyway between Essex Street East and Fleet Street. Map 5.26.

TERRY KELLY'S ("Counterparts": 84)

Terry Kelly, pawn broker, 48 Fleet Street. Map 5.26.

THEATRE ROYAL ("The Dead": 179)

Royal Theatre and Opera House, home of the Dublin Theatre Company, 15 Hawkins Street, on the corner of Poolbeg Street. Map 5.26.

THINGMOTE (*PORTRAIT*: 167)

A green where the Danes assembled outside the precincts of their ninth-century Dublin settlement. It was located in what is now the vicinity of College Green and Suffolk Street, probably where St Andrew's Church now stands. Map 3.15.

THOMAS STREET ("Grace": 144)

The London and Newcastle Tea Co. at 61 Thomas Street may explain Mr Kernan's visit there to "book an order", as well as his movement in the "Wandering Rocks" chapter of *Ulysses*. *Map 6.29.*

TIVOLI ("Counterparts": 85)

The Tivoli Theatre (formerly the Lyric Theatre of Varieties) at 12-13 Burgh Quay. Map 5.26.

TOLKA (*PORTRAIT*: 162)

Rising in Co. Meath about eighteen miles from Dublin, the River Tolka flows south-east and then east by Dunboyne, Clonee, Blanchardstown and Glasnevin. It passes just south of Millbourne Lane where the Joyce family lived in 1894 and flows under the Drumcondra Road, the Ballybough Road, and then the North Strand Road at Annesley Bridge where it empties into Dublin Bay. Map 1.1.

TRINITY COLLEGE ("Two Gallants": 48; "The Dead": 188, *PORTRAIT*: 180)

Trinity occupies an area originally the old Augustinian Monastery of All Hallows or All Saints, built in the twelfth century by the King of Leinster. The land reverted to the Crown at the dissolution and was subsequently given to the city of Dublin for services rendered during the rebellion of Silken Thomas Fitzgerald. The university was chartered by Queen Elizabeth I in 1561 and built on land donated by the city. The present main front was built in 1760 altering the college's earlier Elizabethan architectural character. The railings mentioned in "Two Gallants" encircle the college separating its grounds from the footpath. The clock is on the front of the arched entryway facing the Bank of Ireland and is clearly visible from the footpath though Lenehan "skips out into the road way" to see it. The Trinity College Gate mentioned in "The Dead" is located on the Great Brunswick (Pearse) Street side. In Joyce's time Trinity still symbolized Protestant domination in the island, but its history revolves around the liveliness of its undergraduates and the eccentrieties of its dons. Map 3.15.

TULLABEG (*PORTRAIT*: 14)

The College of St Stanislaus located at Tullabeg had been established during penal times as an elementary school and then became a preparatory school for Clongowes. It was a fine school and trained many future priests and teachers. Some of the masters at Clongowes and at Belvedere had also been at Tullabeg. Crippled by debt, it was amalgamated with Clongowes in 1886.

UNDERDONE'S (*PORTRAIT:* 97)

Joyce refers to the Burlington Hotel and Oyster House (also called "Corless's") just across the street from Foster Place at 26-7 St Andrew's Street and 6 Church Lane. Map 5.25.

USHER'S ISLAND ("The Dead": 160)

Originally an actual island cut off from south Dublin by the flow of the Liffey, the construction of quays narrowed the river and brought it into the south bank. In its earliest days it had been the site of the School of the Friar's Preachers; by Joyce's time, it was the location of the Misses Flynn school where young ladies studied voice and piano and learned polite behaviour. Map 6.29.

VICTORIA HOTEL (*PORTRAIT*: 88)

In *A Portrait* Stephen and his father stay at the Victoria Hotel on St Patrick Street during their trip to Cork. Map 2.9.

VITRIOL WORKS ("An Encounter: 18)

The Dublin and Wicklow Manure Company, vitriol and bleaching liquor manufacturers. Annesley Bridge. Map 4.21.

WARD OF DAWSON STREET ("Ivy Day": 120)

Ernest Ward, solicitor and commissioner for oaths, did not have his office on Dawson Street but nearby at 13 Clare Street. Map 5.24.

WATERHOUSE'S CLOCK ("Two Gallants": 46)

Waterhouse and Company, Gold and Silversmiths at 25-26 Dame Street. The clock used letters instead of numerals to show the time, spelling out H. Waterhouses with the final E at 12 o'clock. Map 5.24.

WEBB'S ("THE DEAD": 170)

George Webb, Bookseller, 5-6 Crampton Quay. Map 5.24.

WELLINGTON MONUMENT ("The Dead": 173)

The 205-foot-high granite obelisk honouring the British general is on the south-east corner of Phoenix Park. Map 7.37.

WESTLAND ROW STATION ("After the Race": 42)

Now Pearse Station, it is located on the corner of Westland Row and Great Brunswick (Pearse) Street. Map 7.36.

WHARF ROAD ("An Encounter": 17)

East Wall Road was popularly known as Wharf Road because of the wharf located there to provide a bathing-place. Map 4.21.

WICKLOW HOTEL (*PORTRAIT*: 11)

6-8 Wicklow Street, Dublin. Map 6.30.

WICKLOW STREET ("Ivy Day": 109)

Maps 5.24 and 6.30.

WINETAVERN STREET ("The Dead": 192)

Map 6.29.

BIBLIOGRAPHY

1. THE TEXTS

A Portrait of the Artist as a Young Man. Edited by Chester G. Anderson and reviewed by Richard Ellmann (New York: The Viking Press, 1964).
Dubliners. Edited by Robert Scholes in consultation with Richard Ellmann (New York: The Viking Press, 1968).
Critical Writings of James Joyce. Edited by Richard Ellmann and Ellsworth Mason (New York: The Viking Press, 1959).
The Letters of James Joyce. Vol. I. Edited by Stuart Gilbert. New York: The Viking Press, 1966. Vols II and III. Edited by Richard Ellmann (New York: The Viking Press, 1966).

2. The Cornell Joyce Collection: CORNELL UNIVERSITY, ITHACA, NEW YORK;

Scholes, Robert E. *The Cornell Joyce Collection: A Catalogue* (Ithaca, 1961).
James Joyce *Alphabetical Notebook* (n.d.).
James Joyce *Manuscript Workbook* (1903).
Letters from Mary Jane Joyce to James Joyce (December 1902 – March 1903). Items 712-17.
Letters from Josephine Murray to James Joyce and to Stanislaus Joyce (1903-20). Items 907-34.

3. Directories, Dictionaries, Maps, Photographs, and Guide Books:
   NATIONAL LIBRARY OF IRELAND COLLECTION, DUBLIN

Araby: the Official Catalogue (1894).
The Belvederian: the Journal of Belvedere College, Vol. I (1907).
Cole and Praeger *Handbook to the City of Dublin* (1908).
Corcoran, Timothy *The Clongowes Record: 1814-1932* (n.d.).
Cosgrave, E.M. and Strangways L. *The Dictionary of Dublin* (1897).
Dignam, James *Dignam's Dublin Guide* (n.d.).
Dictionary of Dublin (1906).
The Directional Pointer Guide Map to Dublin (1900).
Dublin: Ireland's Capital, the Official Guidebook (1924).
Dublin United Tramways Co.: Dublin Street Guide (1941).
Guy, Francis *City and County of Cork Directory* (1894).
Illustrated Guide to Dublin (1902).
Lawrence Collection (Photographs).
Official Guide to Galway and Mayo (1958).
Pettit, S. F. *This City of Cork: 1700-1900* (n.d.).
Road Maps of Ireland (1844).
Thom's Business Directory of Dublin (1906).
Thom's Official Directory of Dublin City and County, 36 vols (1875-1910).
Ward and Lock Guide to Dublin (c. 1900).

4. BIOGRAPHICAL SOURCES

Beebe, Maurice 'Joyce and Stephen Dedalus: The Problem of Autobiography' in *A James Joyce Mis-
   cellany*, ed. Marvin Magalaner (Carbondale, Illinois, 1959).
Byrne, J.F. *Silent Years: An Autobiography with Memoirs of James Joyce and Our Ireland* (New York,
   1953).
Colum, Mary *Life and the Dream* (New York, 1947).
Colum, Padraic *The Road Round Ireland* (New York, 1926).
Colum, Padraic 'Introduction' to Joyce's *Dubliners* (New York: Modern Library, 1929).
Colum, Padraic and Colum, Mary *Our Friend James Joyce* (New York, 1958).
Ellmann, Richard *James Joyce* (New York, 1959).
Ellmann, Richard 'The Limits of Joyce's Naturalism', *The Sawanee Review*, LXIII (Autumn 1955),
   567-75.
Gorman, Herbert *James Joyce: His First Forty Years* (New York, 1940).
Joyce, Stanislaus 'The Background to *Dubliners*', *The Listener*, LI (25 March, 1954), 526-7.
Joyce, Stanislaus *The Dublin Diary*, ed. George H. Healey (London, 1962).
Joyce, Stanislaus 'Joyce's Dublin', *Partisan Review*, XIX (January-Febrruay 1952), 103-9.
Joyce, Stanislaus *My Brother's Keeper*, ed. Richard Ellmann (New York, 1958).
Joyce, Stanislaus *Recollections of James Joyce by His Brother* (New York, 1950).
Magalaner, Marvin 'James Mangan and Joyce's Dedalus Family', *Philological Quarterly*, XXXI (October
   1952), 363-71.
Pascal, Roy 'The Autobiographical Novel and the Autobiography', *Essays in Criticism*, IX (April 1959),
   134-50.
Sullivan, Kevin *Joyce Among the Jesuits* (New York, 1958).
Troy, William 'Stephen Dedalus and James Joyce', *The Nation*, CXXXVIII (14 February, 1934), 187-8.

5. TOPOGRAPHICAL SOURCES

Anderson, Chester K. *James Joyce and His World* (London, 1967).
Ball, F.E. *A History of the County Dublin*, Vols I-IV (Dublin, 1902-20).
Carte, Thomas *The Story of Dublin* (London, 1907).
Colum, Padraic 'Dublin in Literature', *Bookman* (London), LXIII (July 1926), 555-61.
Cosgrave, Dillon *North Dublin, City and Environs* (Dublin, 1909; reprinted Four Courts Press, Dublin,
   1977).
Craig, Maurice *Dublin 1660-1860: A Social and Architectural History* (London, 1952; reprinted Allen
   Figgis, Dublin, 1969).
Curran, Constantine 'When James Joyce Lived in Dublin', *Vogue*, CIX (May 1947), 144-9.
Finegan, John *The Story of Monto* (Cork, 1978).
Fitzpatrick, Samuel *Dublin: A Historical and Topographical Account of the City* (London, 1907).
Haliday, Charles *The Scandinavian Kingdom of Dublin* (Dublin, 1881).
Harvey, John *Dublin: A Study of Environment* (London, 1949).
Hill's Guide to Blackrock (Dublin, 1892; reprinted Carraig Books, Blackrock, 1976).
Huttchins, Patricia *James Joyce's Dublin* (London, 1950).

Huttchins, Patricia *James Joyce's World* (London, 1957).

Joyce, Weston St John *The Neighbourhood of Dublin* (Dublin, 1912).

Kain, Richard M. *Dublin in the Age of William Butler Yeats and James Joyce* (Devon, 1972).

Mac Manus, Seamus *The Story of the Irish Race* (Connecticut, 1979).

Macneill, Eoin *Celtic Ireland* (Dublin, 1981).

McCready, C.T. *Dublin Street Names Dated and Explained* (Dublin, 1892).

Tindall, William York *The Joyce Country* (New York, 1972).

Wood, Tom 'A Portrait of the Artist According to His Dwellings' in *Ulysses: Fifty Years*, ed. Thomas Staley (Bloomington, Indiana, 1974).

6. SELECTED CRITICISM

Bradsher, Frieda "The Use of Place in 'The Dead' ", *Graduate English Papers* (Arizona), 6, i, 26-7.

Cowan, S.A. 'Joyce's Clay', *Explicator*, XXIII, 7 (1965), item 50.

Daiches, David 'Dubliners' in *Twentieth Century Interpretations of 'Dubliners'*, ed. Peter K. Garrett (Englewood Cliffs, New Jersey, 1968).

Gifford, Don *Notes for Joyce: 'Dubliners' and 'A Portrait aof the Artist as a Young Man' (New York, 1967).*

Ghiselin, Brewster 'The Unity of *Dubliners*' in *Twentieth Century Interpretations of 'Dubliners'*, ed. Peter K. Garrett (Englewood Cliffs, New Jersey, 1968).

Halper, Nathan 'The Name Maria', *James Joyce Quarterly*, XII (1975), 303-6.

Halper, Nathan 'The Grave of Michael Bodkin', *James Joyce Quarterly*, XII (1975), 273.

Jones, David E. 'Spatial Relations in Joyce's *Portrait*', Ball State University Forum, 17, ix (1976), 37-40.

Kaye, Julian B. 'Who is Betty Byrne?', *Modern Language Notes*, LXXI (February 1956), 93-5.

Kenner, Hugh *Dublin's Joyce* (Bloomington, Indiana, 1956).

Kenner, Hugh *The Pound Era* (Los Angeles, 1971).

Kopper, Edward "Joyce's 'The Dead'", *Explicator*, XXVI, 6 (1968), item 46.

Levin, Richard and Shattuck, Charles 'First Flight to Ithaca' in *James Joyce: Two Decades of Criticism*, ed. Seon Givens (New York, 1948).

Magalaner, Marvin and Kain Richard M. *Joyce, the Man, the Work, the Reputation.* (New York, 1956).

Magalaner, Marvin and Kain, Richard M. *Times of Apprenticeship: The Fiction of Young James Joyce* (New York, 1959).

McGuinness, Arthur 'The Ambience of Space in Joyce's *Dubliners*', *Studies in Short Fiction*, XI (1974), 343-51.

O'Mahony, Eoin 'Father Conmee and His Associates', *James Joyce Quarterly*, IV (1967), 263.

O'Neill, M.I. 'The Joyces in the Holloway Diaries' in *A James Joyce Miscellany*, ed. Marvin Magalaner (Carbondale, Illinois, 1959).

Pearce, Donald R. 'My Dead King: the Dinner Quarrel in Joyce's *Portrait of the Artist*', *Modern Language Notes*, LXVI (April 1951), 249-51.

Peterson, Richard F. 'Joyce's Use of Time in *Dubliners*', Ball State University Forum, 14, i (1973), 43-51.

Power, Mary 'The Naming of Kathleen Kearney', *Journal of Modern Literature*, V (1975), 552-4.

Raleigh, John Henry 'Afoot in Dublin in Search of the Habitations of Some Shades', *James Joyce Quarterly*, VIII (1971), 129-41.

Scholes, Robert and Kain Richard M. *The Workshop of Daedalus: James Joyce and the Raw Materials for "A Portrait of the Artist as a Young Man"* (Evanston, Illinois, 1965).

Sider, David '"Counterparts" and the *Odyssey*', *James Joyce Quarterly*, VIII (1971), 182-4.

Solomon, Albert J. 'The Backgrounds of "Eveline"', *Eire*, VI, 3 (1970), 23-8.

Torchiana, Donald T. 'Joyce's "Two Gallants": A Walk through the Ascendancy', *James Joyce Quarterly*, VI (1968), 115-27.

Torchiana, Donald T. 'Joyce's "After the Race", the Races of Castlebar, and Dun Laoghaire', *Eire*, 6, iii (1971), 119-28.

Torchiana, Donald T. 'Joyce's "Eveline" and the Blessed Margaret Mary Alacoque', *James Joyce Quarterly*, VI (1968), 22-8.

Van Voorhis, John W. 'The Smoothing Iron: A Topographical Note to "An Encounter"', *James Joyce Quarterly*, X (1973), 266.

West, Michael 'Old Cotter and the Enigma of Joyce's "The Sisters"', *Modern Philology*, 67 (1970), 370-2.

DATE DUE